BALANCING WORK AND HOME

A Practical Guide to Managing Stress

A Parents at Work Publication

Parents at Work/ The Working Mothers Association
77 Holloway Road, London N7 8JZ
071-700 5771

Registered Charity no. 295217

ISBN 0 9508792 9 0

Edited by Sarah Litvinoff and Lucy Daniels
Text by Kay Marles
Cartoons by Sophie Grillet

British Library Cataloguing-in-Publication Data. A catalogue record for this book is available from the British Library.

Printed and bound in Great Britain by
Biddles Ltd, Guildford and King's Lynn

Acknowledgements
With grateful thanks to Brenda Brodie, Mandy Cass, Patricia Cleghorn of the Self Esteem Company, Susie Courtault of Maternity Matters, Veronica Davies, Bill Garlick, Judith Harrison, Lydia Hearst, Jenny Hildreth, Wendy Jennings, Suzan E. Lewis, Susan McDougall, Lynn Marshall, Sue Mills, Linda Severne, Tom Smith, Hilary Simpson, Sarah Wyndham-Lewis. Special thanks to Shell, and the personnel at Shell who helped with their expertise; and to all the people who have been quoted anonymously, for giving their time and speaking so frankly about their experiences.

Finally, we are grateful to **Shell** for their generous support in funding this publication.

CONTENTS

INTRODUCTION

'If you want something done, ask a busy woman.' This maxim could have been coined for working mothers. Life as a working parent is hectic, but the challenge can stretch you in the most satisfying way. The sheer number of things to be done develops your efficiency and resourcefulness and combining work with parenting increases your wisdom, responsibility and maturity too. No wonder employers are waking up to the fact that parents on the payroll are a valuable asset, not a liability.

Contrary to popular belief, balancing work and home is not a new phenomenon. Previous generations of women have gone out to work in factories, mills, hospitals, schools and offices, or they have taken in work to do at home, while their children have been looked after by older siblings, grandmothers, aunts, sisters-in-law or neighbours; and all the while they have continued to run the home, manage the money, and take on responsibility for the majority of domestic tasks. Nowadays this dual responsibility is also being undertaken by men, who previously felt work was their province and children and home were the responsibility of their wives.

Many mothers used to work out of financial necessity and continue to do so today. But women work for other reasons too: the enjoyment and stimulation of an interesting job; the satisfaction of contributing something and of being seen as a person in her own right; the value of having an independent income; the desire to use talents and skills; the boost to esteem and self confidence and the companionship of colleagues. These good feelings can be passed on to partners and children by mothers who feel fulfilled. Similarly, fathers who now involve themselves more in home matters find that this adds a new dimension to their feelings about themselves and their perspective at work.

Even though the balancing act is not new, it is no easier today. Working parents who get it right however, speak of a sense of achievement and excitement:

'On a good day I have the sneaking suspicion that I do have the best of both worlds, that I am having my cake and eating it too'.

This satisfaction is increased by watching your children grow up having benefited from the situation:

'At nineteen she shows all the positive qualities of a child brought up by a mother who worked. She's independent, responsible, with masses of initiative. We protect our children, but foster any small spark of independence at the right time, because the more they can take responsibility for themselves, the more we can cut from our own list of duties. Looking back I can say that she gained something from all her childcare experiences - childminder, nursery, out-of-school care. Perhaps it was lucky that she was a bright, robust child who loved company and a variety of experiences. Or perhaps the situation created these qualities. Who can say?'

But inevitably there are times when the balance goes wrong, or when both ends of the scale seem too heavily weighted; times when arrangements break down or the emotional mix gets too much or the feelings of achievement become overshadowed by tiredness. This is when we start to experience stress. Stress is something most of us would like to cut out of our lives because it can be debilitating. At work, it is thought to trigger a range of ailments, both physical and mental. At home, it can leave us without energy for our most important relationships.

But not all stress is bad, and stress is not all bad. It comes about as a result of being busy and in demand, because we are living varied and interesting lives. On one level, it warns us to slow down and relax. On another, it can make us work more efficiently, provide inspiration and give us just the kick-start we need.

Feeling under pressure tends to come and go at different times in our lives. A teacher interviewed for this book while she was on half-term was relaxed and positive about the effects of stress on her life; six weeks later, with the full weight of disciplinary problems, marking, preparation, and her own children's school lives on top of her, stress was right at the top of her emotional chart.

Fortunately we don't have to feel victims of stress. There are many ways in which we can handle it, use it to give us energy and focus, or reduce it to manageable proportions.

This book aims to put you in control. All the working parents interviewed on the following pages said they felt stressed at times, but none would radically change their lives. They spoke about the buzz and the sense of satisfaction that comes from raising a family and pursuing a career.

'My mother, who never worked outside the home, passed on feelings of frustration,' said one mother of two. 'I feel enormously happy to be able to do my job and have a family, and I know that with any other arrangement I'd be worse off.'

Cutting stress out of your life completely is impossible because stress is about being alive. But if you recognise the warning signs you can take action, and manage the delicate balancing act between work and home.

WHY ARE YOU BALANCING WORK AND HOME?

When things get on top of you it is easy to forget all the positive aspects of combining home and work. Use this checklist to remind yourself of why you do it!

☐ *Having some money to call my own*

☐ *More money for family necessities*

☐ *Building a career for myself*

☐ *Intellectual stimulation from my work*

☐ *Getting out, mixing with people*

☐ *Time when I'm 'me' - not a partner or parent*

☐ *I enjoy my job*

☐ *Bringing a new perspective into the home*

☐ *Knowing my children value the time we spend together*

Now list the three things you would miss most about combining work and home - either from the checklist or other ideas of your own. Keep it to look at when things get too much.

1.

2.

3.

1. STRESS: WHAT IT FEELS LIKE, WHY IT HAPPENS

'I'd found someone who seemed like the ideal childminder, a former nurse whose house was on my way to work, but on the day I was due to go back, she phoned to say she didn't think she could look after my daughter after all.'

'My daughter won't do her homework until I get home at 6 o'clock. That means that into the next two hours we have to cram in talking about school, doing her homework, having tea, having a bath and getting ready for bed. My husband isn't usually there, and it's the time of day when I feel most tired.'

'I'm locked into an expensive mortgage and can't afford to lose my job. But now I'm a single parent, it is getting increasingly hard to combine care for my two school-age boys with the long hours and travel that I'm expected to put in at work. Maybe because I'm a man, my employers forget that I have domestic responsibilities too and, in the current economic climate, I daren't ask for concessions. This business is traditionally stressful - you either put up with it or get out.'

Such dramas are characteristic of our day and age, but stress is something that would have affected cave man himself. In any situation that threatens us or takes us by surprise, we tend to react as he would have done, with 'fight or flight' instincts: that is, wanting either to square up and fight, or to do the opposite and run away. In both cases the body responds by gearing up for action, and that makes your heart pound, your head race and your energy levels go up a notch or two.

Rarely today do we get the chance to respond to those instincts however. There are laws to prevent us from bashing up the childminder who has let us down, and that stop us running away from the mortgage repayments. It is having to suppress the energy that has been whipped up that causes the physical symptoms associated with stress: breathlessness, rapid heartbeat, tension.

The way you handle the experience depends partly on your personality. What can be unbearably demanding for one person may be exhilarating to another. Stress researchers have separated out two main types: Type A tend to be aggressive, always in a rush, workaholics, high achieving, and restless. When something goes wrong they are immediately on the alert and their stress levels rise, yet they are energised by situations that are manageably demanding. Type B are the opposite: laid back, good listeners, not so inclined to hurry or worry. When the pressure is on they tend not to panic and take it in their stride, yet they can't handle too much activity and excitement.

Two further factors affect your ability to cope: hardiness and the extent to which you feel in control. If you are hardy - healthy physically and mentally - you are better able to cope with pressure. With this also comes confidence and perhaps a sense of responsibility and a positive attitude to change. If you feel in control you are likely to take for granted that you can influence the course of your life - feel that you are a driver rather than a passenger. This means that when crises arise you look for a solution rather than feel swamped.

Whatever your ability to cope, stressful situations will arise. These are the kinds of experiences everyone can recognise:

- Short-term frustrations, such as being kept waiting at the doctor's surgery when you are expected at work, or suddenly having to take the day off because your childcarer falls ill.

- Long-term pressures, such as poor working relationships, weeks of adhering to a fixed timetable, or continuing problems with childcare.

- Demands that come and go, such as having to work very hard at the end of each month to get invoices out, or worries about keeping your children busy and safe in the school holidays.

When stress works for you

- It is good when it acts as a stimulant, so that you enjoy the variety in what you do. To this end you contrive to organise matters so that you achieve more, which gives you confidence.

- It is good if it makes you work harder, leading to greater job satisfaction or more time at home. Working to meet a deadline can make you more organised and efficient, and help you to focus your ideas.

- It is good if it stops you procrastinating or from being lethargic, both of which are frustrating.

When stress becomes too much

- Instead of being happily active you try to cram too much in, and find you do it less efficiently. It is harder to take decisions, or know what you are aiming for.

- You become unable to stay on top of things and lose your sense of perspective. You start but don't finish jobs at home or at work, and the undone tasks haunt you.

- You become more irritable, at home and at work, and lose your patience more often. Things that would have amused you before now worry you.

- At worst, you feel trapped and lonely and long to be rescued.

I'M TRYING TO REMEMBER WHAT IT IS ABOUT MY JOB THAT I LOVE SO MUCH

WARNING SIGNS

No one needs to tell you when you are under pressure - your workload and the anxiety you feel speak for themselves. But when should you take stock and do something about it? The following is a list of symptoms that you should regard as warning signs which tell you that you should rethink and reschedule.

- You have more headaches than normal

- You feel constantly tired

- You have trouble sleeping

- Your appetite goes, or you crave comfort food

- Your digestion suffers: you experience nausea, constipation or diarrhoea

- You're jumpy and suffer cramp, muscle spasms or nervous twitches

- Your heart races more than usual

- You are often sweaty or breathless

Taken in isolation, one or two of these symptoms should not worry you. But too many of them over too long a period lower your resistance and can make you prone to illness and depression.

WHAT CAUSES STRESS

There are as many causes of stress as there are individuals, but some pressures have been identified as being particularly hard to handle for everyone.

- Change is demanding, whether it is moving house or starting a new job; settling your child with a carer or your child starting school; earning less money or even receiving a promotion; tackling a different journey to work or a new area of responsibility in your job. It doesn't matter whether the change is pleasant or difficult, the mere fact of having to do things differently - and consequently give your energy and attention to what you could previously do automatically - is wearing. It is often the number of changes you have to cope with at one time that matters. One or two together might be manageable, more and you feel overloaded.

- Time Pressure. Simply having more to do than you can reasonably cope with for longer than brief periods takes its toll. When this involves being in a constant rush, whether at home, in the car or at work, you naturally become tense.

- Caring For Others. The joy and satisfaction you get from having children is accompanied by the normal responsibilities and worries they can also bring. At difficult times, especially if you have elderly relatives to consider as well, the role of the carer can be demanding.

- Unrealistic Aims. Many images of parenthood present ideals, which are very different from reality. Trying to live up to these makes for unnecessary self-induced pressure. Similarly, having rigid, over-ambitious goals for yourself at work can mean you drive yourself too hard.

Quite apart from these are the normal concerns and problems of daily living: worrying about being ill or coping with sickness; anxiety about your children's safety; and larger worries about the state of the world. Any additional problems that arise, such as coping with bureaucracy or legal entanglements, can turn out to be the last straw. Inevitably, once you start looking, there are pressures everywhere! Fortunately they don't usually all descend at once, and even at difficult times finding different ways to cope or looking for ways to ease the pressure can make all the difference.

The next chapter looks at ways you can help yourself.

YOUR OWN BEST FRIEND OR YOUR OWN WORST ENEMY?

Answer the following questions truthfully: are they true (T), false (F) or sometimes true (S)?

- *It is important to me to do everything perfectly.*

- *I feel guilty when I am not doing something useful.*

- *I don't like saying no when people ask me to do them a favour, or give me extra work.*

- *I worry a lot, even about things I can't influence.*

- *I find it difficult to ask for help or sympathy.*

- *I push myself hard, even when I feel ill.*

- *I think saying that you have too much to do is an admission of failure.*

- *I think it is normal to feel tired all the time.*

- *If my partner wants to rest in the evening I'll do everything, even if I long to put my feet up too.*

- *When I'm at work I worry about home; when I'm at home I worry about work.*

If you say 'true' or 'sometimes true' to any of these statements, then you are contributing to your over-work and feelings of stress. Look at them again and imagine what you would have to do and how you would have to behave if you answered 'false' instead.

2. KEEPING THE BALANCE

'I do lock myself in the bathroom, and I have spent an occasional day on a watercolour course which is wonderfully relaxing. But working is part of my way of creating me-time and as well as having two children and a full-time job, I have also got myself onto several committees.'

This woman's way of organising her life might sound like heaven or hell to you. The point is that she has discovered what suits her, and is happier and more fulfilled because of it. In the same way, by taking control of the elements of your life and making them work for you rather than against you, it is possible to start to feel less harrassed and pressured from today.

SELF HELP

Manage your time

- Give yourself an over-view of what you do by listing the tasks you try to fit into an average day. Be prepared for it to be very long! Look at it objectively. Put a tick by the things you really have to do and a question mark by those that you think you ought to do. Could you delegate any of these - or eliminate them altogether?

- Look again at your list of essentials. If they are very time-consuming you should question your standards. Are you trying to keep a perfect home, or cook elaborate meals, when some corner-cutting would perhaps be better? Ask yourself who says you should be perfect?

- A list-making habit can help you streamline more generally. List what you plan to do today. If you regularly can't finish the items on your list it means you are planning to do too much.

- Break down larger tasks into manageable stages, and set realistic targets. Build in a time allowance for things to take longer than you estimate.

- Try not to procrastinate. Getting on with a job makes you feel on top of things. If you keep putting it off, cut it out altogether.

THERE — I'VE EVEN SQUEEZED IN 2½ MINUTES FOR REST AND RECREATION

DAILY SCHEDULE

Sophie

● Draw a circle and divide it into segments showing how much time you spend on various activities in an average week. For instance, a slice for time at work, one for commuting, one for housework, one for cooking, one for time with the children, and so on. Include any hobbies or activities you enjoy. Then draw a second circle, using the same headings, representing how you would prefer to spend your time, by making the relevant sections larger or smaller. It could be quite major, such as making the work slice smaller and time with children larger: then you know that perhaps you need to aim towards reducing your hours. But sometimes less radical changes make all the difference. One person discovered a large 'television' slice and a tiny 'reading' slice - yet much preferred reading. Another saw that housework was taking up more time than more pleasurable activities, and looked for ways to cut this down.

Keep healthy

The better shape you are in physically, the more able you are to cope with having a busy lifestyle.

15

- Eat well Convenience foods are often essential, but choose the healthier ones. Raw fruit and vegetables are good for you and quick to prepare. Cut down on tea and coffee - caffeine is a stressor - and drink more plain water or mineral water.

- Take exercise It's a good way of winding down and it also strengthens you. Choose something you like: a regular long walk, swimming, playing sport or going to the gym. In the USA people are taking up 'executive boxing' to help alleviate stress!

Make me-time

- It's important to set aside time every day to use exactly as you want. It may be as brief as a long bath in the evening, or a quick drink with a friend when the children are in bed: space for you to look forward to when no one will be making demands on you.

- Take it in turns with your partner to look after the children for an hour or half a day or more. When it's your turn, go out and do whatever makes you feel good: some shopping; a favourite sport; having your hair done; an evening out with friends; or shut yourself away and do whatever you most feel like at the time, including absolutely nothing. If you don't have a partner see if you can make a similar arrangement with a friend or neighbour.

  'Recently I had a whole day to myself and I went out taking photographs which I really enjoyed.'

- Designate some worry time. It sounds strange, but it works! If you worry a great deal, set aside a time once a week when you address your worries. If you catch yourself brooding at other times, remind yourself to put the worry out of your mind until the official time.

Treat yourself

It is surprising how few people feel happy with the idea of rewarding themselves. The point is, however small the treat, doing something to make you feel good relegates problems and pressures to the background for a while and puts them in proportion.

- Make a list of all the things you enjoy and which help you to relax. It can include gardening; eating chocolate; watching a funny video; talking to a friend you haven't seen for ages, and so on. Keep your list handy, and make sure you do them!

'My partner and I take it in turns to have an occasional day or weekend to "drop out" of domestic routine. I like browsing in bookshops and usually come home with a pile of new thrillers or cookery books. Barbara's idea of a treat is getting her hair done or escaping city life for the country for a couple of days.'

● Buy yourself small treats - something that's just for you. It could be flowers or something else that takes your fancy. Treating yourself is a way of showing you value yourself.

● Make an event out of your treats: have your bath by candlelight, for instance, and scent it with reviving or relaxing essential oils. Planning to introduce more pure pleasure into your life can become as habitual as worrying - only more healthy!

'One advantage of working odd hours is that I can make space for myself. I might go for a turkish bath or a swim. I know when I need to take a break and it always helps.'

Think positive

● Don't get caught up in the prospect of all you have to do. plan things to look forward to: days out or holidays. Choose things that meet your needs - to have fun with the family, wind down and relax, or be active if it makes you feel good.

'We resist getting things too planned at the weekend. There have been Sundays when none of us gets dressed until lunchtime. The kids watch cartoons, we read the papers. It is a break from our usual regime and a let-up that we all look forward to.'

● Enjoy the good moments - every day has them - don't spoil them by worrying about problems.

● Get problems in perspective. They don't last forever. Note down the steps you can take to tackle them. Then forget them until you have to take action.

● Make sure there is laughter in your life. As well as being a good method of evaluating - if you can't laugh at something it really is serious - it is good for general well being and helps you relax.

- Forget perfection; striving for it is stressful in itself. Pat yourself on the back for what you have achieved - you are doing great! Don't concentrate on your shortcomings.

  'Sometimes I work late at night to get something finished to a deadline. The adrenalin gives me a high. But the best thing is the achievement of doing something like that without the world falling apart.'

- Don't blame others. Developing personal responsibility for your own actions will help you keep control of your own life. If you say things such as, 'It runs in the family. My father was just like me' you are being passive and shifting responsibility onto others. Try to be positive: 'I can choose how to react. I don't have to let things upset me.'

- Develop flexibility - about your own methods and those of others. Being too rigid creates stress when things don't go to plan. It doesn't matter how it gets done, so long as it gets done!

- Become more assertive: learning to say no puts you back in control (more about this in chapter 4).

- Combat any feelings of being powerless by becoming involved. Joining a local health committee, for example, can give you a voice, and put you in the know. But don't take on extras like this out of guilt - it's counter-productive.

Find support

- It's not all down to you. Friends, family, partners, colleagues can all be encouraged or cajoled into helping or offering sympathy or an ear.

- Find like-minded people. A working parents' group at work or in the neighbourhood can offer support, understanding and practical help. There is no virtue in coping alone, but reluctance to admit that you might need help can be holding you back.

  'I have a group of friends who work for the same company and who all have children. We keep in touch and sometimes have lunch together on a Saturday. We are friends because we are in the same situation. We worked together before we had our children, but now we have become very close.'

Learn to relax

There's more to relaxing than sitting down with a cup of coffee for ten minutes. Learning to unwind wherever you are by switching off and relaxing your muscles helps avoid unnecessary fatigue and lowers anxiety levels before a demanding event.

● The following is an all-purpose relaxation exercise that you can do for yourself in a spare 5 minutes:

Sit in a comfortable chair, though an upright one is fine as well. Make sure there will be no interruptions. Close your eyes. Breathe out deeply, and then in; breathe out again, slowly and deeply; continue for as long as the time you have available.

As you establish this slow rhythmic breathing pattern concentrate on different parts of your body and feel them relax. Start with the feet and work your way up. Think about each part, not just the feet but the toes too. If you find your mind wandering and becoming active, stop and go back to the beginning. Listen to your breathing. When you reach your forehead, you can concentrate on the sensation of feeling relaxed all over and enjoying the accompanying quiet and calm. Focus on this for the rest of the time available. When you have finished, yawn, open your eyes slowly and do some slow shaking out movements before getting up.

With practice, you will find this exercise becoming more and more effective. Initially, it can help to plan time for it every day, until you can do it with confidence at different times and in different places.

GETTING HELP

In the previous pages, we looked at some of the ways that you can manage your time and make space for some relaxation, be it sports activities or just enjoying half an hour's peace listening to your favourite record.

When you have a demanding job and a family to look after too (which may include elderly relatives or a sick partner as well as children) it is easy to forget that you also need some 'tender, loving care'! Time for yourself or - even better - being pampered by someone else, will give you the strength you need to sustain your caring role.

Listed below are some other methods of 'caring' for yourself - they may not all be relevant - but there is no shortage of choice to meet a variety of needs!

Practical methods, therapies and treatments

Many complementary therapies can help you relax or deal with the effects of stress. Some of them definitely come into the category of treats. The Institute for Complementary Therapies (see Chapter 8) is a good starting point for detailed information. This is a brief look at some of what is on offer. Regular treatments require time, planning and commitment. Some of them are costly. The important thing is to choose a method that appeals to you. The benefits can have a knock-on effect. Taking up yoga, for example, can relax you and make you feel good; you are likely to go home to your partner and children refreshed and in a positive frame of mind.

Hypnotherapy In a state of altered awareness, you may be asked to imagine stress-inducing situations and become receptive to suggestions for remaining calm and relaxed in similar situations.

Biofeedback Uses electronic machines to pinpoint certain physiological functions in the body. For example, it may locate the muscle tension that is causing a headache. By watching the monitor you then learn how to alter physiological responses to prevent stress building up.

Autogenic training Autogenic training is a form of hypnosis that accesses the unconscious while not fully asleep. It can be used for creative problem solving and implanting positive ideas.

Creative visualisation Creative Visualisation is the art of using your imagination to visualise goals you want to achieve. Focussing on images in the mind is thought to supply the body with a creative get up and go.

Cognitive restructuring Teaches how to look anew at what you and others do and say. It is often the basis for stress management courses.

Meditation	Meditation is an age old method of relaxing, and with practice can lead to a calmer approach to life. It involves sitting very quietly, concentrating deeply on one word or object and breathing deeply. People who do it often find it the best part of their day.

Body treatments

Acupuncture	This Chinese medicinal treatment involves inserting tiny needles into acupuncture points in the body to restore the body's balance according to each individual's make-up, lifestyle and constitution.
Alexander Technique	Alexander Technique is concerned with teaching an improved physical posture which stops unnecessary body tension, thus relieving stress.
Aromatherapy	A relaxing therapy with a high feel-good factor, aromatherapists use essential oils and face and body massage.
Herbalism	Herbal remedies from this country or traditional Chinese herbs are regarded as valuable in treating tension, depression and anxiety.
Homeopathy	The homeopath takes all aspects of your personality and life style into account when recommending a remedy, which stimulates the symptoms to help the body to help itself.
Massage	Massage is good for relaxing muscles and relieving pain particularly in the back and shoulders, and gives you a sense of well being.
Osteopathy	Osteopaths use light finger massage to bring about realignments and alleviate complaints such as backache.
Reflexology	Reflex points on the feet or hands are massaged to help reduce stress and harmonise parts of the body.
Shiatsu	Shiatsu is a form of massage therapy which concentrates on the pressure points and meridians in the body.
Yoga	Yoga teaches exercise in a gentle and controlled way, through postures, movements and breathing exercises and can induce a deep state of relaxation. Yoga is usually taught in groups.

Counselling and therapies

Counselling   Counsellors are trained to listen but not to judge. They help clients see anxieties in a new light and possibly identify a new way of dealing with them.

Psychotherapy   Deals with real life problems by looking into the unconscious for deep rooted motives and fears.

Group therapy   Group therapy is similar but it is cheaper and individuals can learn by listening to others.

Family therapy   All members of a family work with a therapist, who observes the family dynamics and treats the family difficulties within the family situation.

These are ways of helping yourself or turning to others for treatment. But what about identifying and dealing with specific problems in your daily life? For many this will include irritations at work. Recognising the crunchpoints is the first step towards dealing with them, and the next chapter helps you do this.

CHECKLIST

- **Anticipate and prepare for difficult moments.**

'I pick my son up from nursery school and then rush home to give him, me and the baby lunch. We are all hungry and time is very short. If I can plan in advance what we are going to eat, and include buying an occasional pizza or something ready-made, I find I can function on automatic pilot.'

- **Reorganise how you divide your time.**

Be ruthless about cutting out anything that is time-consuming, disagreeable and not strictly necessary, and substitute something you enjoy, or even a good rest.

'I've splashed out on a cleaner once a week for two hours to do the really dirty jobs. It's my best buy of any week. It frees me to do other things, and I still get a buzz when I come home from work on the cleaner's day to see things sparkling.'

- **Make sure you have enough support.**

Ask yourself: Who can I rely on to help out with the children in an emergency? Who can I talk to about work problems? Who can I talk to about my children without boring them? Which neighbour is prepared to lend a hand from time to time? Who makes me feel good about myself? Who can I really laugh and unwind with?

The more variety of names you have, the more supported you will feel. Perhaps it's your mother who will listen endlessly about your children, your best old schoolfriend you laugh most heartily with, a trusted colleague you talk to about work, and so on. Remember they are more likely to be there for you if you reciprocate.

'When doing the list I felt I could put my partner in every category. But sometimes it seems unfair. When things are difficult I can see I'm burdening him by unloading all the time. That's when I pop next door and moan to Ellie instead.'

3. DEMANDS AT WORK

'I enjoy my work and feel that the whole family has benefited, not only financially, but through my peace of mind at having fulfilled my ambitions and having some independence.'

This remark is typical of what women returners say. For men and women, work at its best is far more than a way of making money. It is stimulating and challenging, and through its demands you can develop talents and abilities you might not have known you had.

That is the up side. The down side is that at times there can be difficulties. Perhaps you are in the wrong job, or have a capricious boss, or there is some upheaval. You need to determine whether this is temporary or more long-term.

The Job

Top of the league table of pressurised careers comes work such as advertising, journalism, being in the police force or an airline pilot - all competitive or demanding of concentration and commitment. Repetitive jobs where you have little control over how you plan your work bring boredom and frustration which can turn into stress too. Work supposed to be least stressful includes beauty therapy, working for a building society or in a museum or library. But these tables can be misleading. A beauty therapist might well feel stretched to the limit if she has a continuous string of appointments with no break. A gentle job in a museum can be wearing if the boss is unpleasant or inflexible. Many other factors will affect how demanding you find your job:

Work overload   Having more work than you can handle on a regular basis.

Work underload   It can occur when you are starting a new job or moving within your organisation and your new role and responsibilities are not yet clear.

'I was jobless for 3 months after returning to work after my third child. I had to go in to be paid. It's the worst three months I've ever had working for the company. I had to grit my teeth to go in every day, thinking I could be at home with my child.'

Emotional involvement	If, at work, you are subject to personal abuse, or involved in disturbing situations, or dealing with illness or even death, it can be difficult to turn off at the end of the day.
Work and free time	Any situation that sets work demands in conflict with your home life can encroach on free time. Meetings can be the biggest bugbears. They may be arranged at times that clash with childcare arrangements or overrun into them; if you work part-time, you find meetings arranged on your day off.
New technology	Continually having to master new systems can be taxing.
Travelling	When your work takes you away from home regularly you might be the envy of your desk-bound friends. But travelling itself is wearing, as is leaving your children.

Daily irritations

These are the annoyances that can be frustrating over a long period.

Organisational structure	Feeling that you are at a lower or higher level than you should be. Feeling cut off from office communications of which you think you should be a part.

NO, I CAN'T TAKE A HOLIDAY THIS YEAR, BUT I'M NOT LETTING IT GET ME DOWN

Unclear responsibilities	Working for someone who gives poor directions, or being asked to do things that are not part of your job description.
Rewards	You think you are not being paid enough, not being given your rightful status or not getting enough job satisfaction.
Promotion	Wanting promotion but knowing that it is unlikely because of your family situation, an unjust appraisal, or other reasons.
Environment	Noise from outside or inside, pollution in its many forms, problems with airconditioning or heating systems, working in cramped conditions, and so on.

'A rather eccentric colleague solved the problem of headaches because of the fluorescent lighting in our new offices by wearing a wide brimmed straw hat at her desk.'

The journey	For working parents the journey often includes dropping children off at a childminder, nursery or school first. Some journeys can be long and difficult, and raise worries about being late.

Work relationships

You don't choose your colleagues, and yet you see more of them than your nearest and dearest.

Daily interaction	A boss can make life hell, ignoring what you say but taking credit for your successes, or by being inconsiderate and inflexible. A subordinate not doing the job well can be a source of irritation; with equals you may find yourself in competition. There may be personality conflicts.
Changes in personnel	A new boss brings changes, and perhaps an entirely different style. New subordinates need to be trained. Even new colleagues on the same level need to be settled in and allowances made for them.
Harassment	Apart from being upsetting or worse, harassment carries additional concerns about how it may affect your job security and promotion prospects. Unless your employer has formal policies and procedures to deal with such matters sypathetically, you may worry about whether to report it or try to deal with it yourself.

Just a cog in the wheel?

Some organisations, especially those with specialised human resource or equal opportunities officers, are developing policies and procedures to help alleviate the problems that arise for employees balancing work with caring responsibilities. Yet, many employers still forget to treat members of staff as individuals with needs. They make inordinate demands on people with responsibilities, such as working parents, and offer no flexibility.

'This can lead to the individual feeling unappreciated, undervalued and stressed,' says a consultant. 'Feeling too insignifcant to make a difference is part of the difficulty.'.

Feeling invisible

You believe all that matters is that the work gets done, and nobody cares or notices if you have difficulties, personal or work-related.

Wanting changes

You know what you would like to change at work but you are nervous about expressing yourself and suspect you will be seen as a troublemaker if you do.

Corporate culture

There appears to be an unwritten policy that 'good' workers work longer than the contracted number of hours.

'There are expectations that one will work after hours, or generally change one's schedule to accommodate demands at work,' says a local government officer. 'That is usually very difficult for working parents who are in some kind of routine. It's almost impossible to organise a routine that's flexible enough to allow for sudden changes.'

Work social life

Going out for a drink after work may be difficult, yet that is often when celebrations happen:

'It felt like a deprivation, not being able to go out to the pub and celebrate a friend's promotion or have a farewell drink when someone left our department,' says a single mother. 'It was completely out of bounds for me. I had no option but to be at the childminder's at a certain time each day and that was that.'

Working patterns

There is good and bad in all working patterns. The trick is to find the one that suits you best. Make the wrong choice, and you increase the pressures on you.

9 to 5

The classic full-time job offers least flexibility if you are trying to combine it with looking after children.

27

Part-time	On the face of it a good solution for parents who want to spend more time with their children. But not if you are disturbed by the rush from work to school, worry about possible loss of pension rights or other benefits and work overtime to overcome your guilt about working part-time!
	You also need to consider how ambitious you are: working part-time can restrict your chance of promotion. Many rights and benefits are closed to part-timers, making your job less secure. Working shorter hours can also mean you have limited opportunities to chat and become part of the gang.
Working shifts	Working different shifts from your partner means that you don't have to pay for childcare, but you see less of each other.
Being on call	In any profession where a bleeper is an essential work tool you cannot easily schedule time to relax.
Working evenings	When your children are young and in bed early, and you have seen them during the day, this might suit you. You can miss out on time with older children, however, or time alone with your partner.
Working weekends	This cuts down on traditional time with the family, which can be hard to make up if they are busy the rest of the week.

'I often have preparation to do on Sundays' says a teacher and father of two. 'It tends to cause conflict because that is when the children want me to do something with them.'

Working from home	Although this can mean more time with the children, it can also mean too much time with them - if they insist on encroaching on your work space and hours. You have nowhere to escape to after a bad day at work. You are already at home!
Self employment	You do not have the financial security of a weekly or monthly pay cheque yet you probably have to pay for childcare on a regular, contractual basis. You never say no to offers of work. You may be frantically busy for days and weeks and then idle.

The new working mother at work

'I had just spent six months with a baby and when I first got back to work, I can remember being amazed that people were listening to me and taking me seriously.'

However good it is to be back, there is always a transition period that needs to be negotiated. Change, as we have seen, is stressful in itself, but there are particular problems with which the new mother may have to contend. The first is missing your child, when you have been in such close contact. You can take time to get back into the rhythm of work, and fear you have lost your touch. Colleagues or superiors who do not approve of working mothers can make you feel guilty.

Case study

Angela works as a technician in a multinational chemical firm. After several years of full-time work she felt cut off when she went on her first maternity leave and her line manager did little to encourage her back. On her return Angela found that the woman covering her maternity leave had taken on her job full-time and she was moved to a different division.

Lack of support during maternity leave and on returning to work can dent anyone's self-esteem and Angela found it helpful to chat to a representative from the Working Mothers Association who suggested she might benefit from joining a local working parents group. None exist where Angela lives and instead she decided to set up a workplace parents group.

The company agreed to promote the group by printing publicity material and publicising its first meeting on notice boards and via electronic mail. The personnel department also helped by inviting mothers on maternity leave to come along to keep in touch with colleagues.

Although setting up the group and helping to keep it organised is an added responsibility (Angela does not get 'official' time to do it) the benefits have been great both for herself, for other employees and the company itself. Angela feels a sense of achievement helping new mothers with their queries about returning to work and finds the shared concerns help to put her own anxieties into perspective. The group has made practical suggestions to management about how they can help working parents and all women going on maternity leave now receive an information pack with contact names in the company and childcare information. The company has benefited from the publicity gained by the group and from the positive feedback from women returners, who settle into work again more easily.

The dual career couple

When both of you work there are clear financial benefits, and you can also appreciate the fresh perspective you bring to the home and to your conversations with each other. Occasionally, however, your careers can come into conflict.

Whose job is more important? When one of you is offered work that means relocating, there can be disagreement about the decision when it means the other having to give up a good job.

Professional rivalry One of you is doing conspicuously better than the other, which causes friction. Should the less successful one be taking on more home responsibilities, or should they still be shared?

Worries for the future

There are less immediate problems that can undermine you, particularly if you are a worrier. These underlying anxieties can make you more cautious about disturbing the status quo or asking for changes at work for fear of drawing unwelcome attention to yourself.

Fear of redundancy Perhaps you have been told that redundancies are in the offing, or you suspect they might be.

Unemployment You think about what you would do if you were out of a job.

'If a man is made redundant, most of the talk is about the loss of the breadwinner. But when it happens to a woman, she may encounter people who think it will be all right for her because her partner works and she can stay at home and be a housewife. A female executive coming across this kind of attitude can be made to feel worthless and without value; there is a sense in which the hard-won right to work crumbles away with the assumption that you'll return happily to the domestic role.'

Retirement Not all parents have their children in their 20s and the prospect of retirement may be well within sight. You may even be looking forward to it, but be concerned about how you will cope and what you will do.

Fortunately, most people only have to grapple with one or two of these problems at once, and there are ways to deal with all of them - or at least lessen their impact. The next chapter contains a range of solutions.

TROUBLESHOOTER

Which problems do you need to address urgently? Look at the statements on this chart and give yourself 0 if it is not a problem; 1 if it bothers you intermittently; and 2 if it is affecting your ability to cope. The ones on which you score 2 are those you need to tackle first.

	0	1	2
I am consistently overworked	☐	☐	☐
I am bored and underemployed	☐	☐	☐
I can't switch off at the end of the day	☐	☐	☐
Work commitments often run into my own time	☐	☐	☐
I have too many new systems to learn	☐	☐	☐
I must travel too often for work	☐	☐	☐
I am not being promoted as I deserve	☐	☐	☐
I have been promoted to a job I can't handle	☐	☐	☐
No one is clear about what my job involves	☐	☐	☐
I am underpaid	☐	☐	☐
I have little job satisfaction	☐	☐	☐
Physical surroundings at work are uncomfortable	☐	☐	☐
My journey to and from work is long/stressful	☐	☐	☐
My boss is difficult	☐	☐	☐
I don't get on with colleagues/subordinates	☐	☐	☐
I am subjected to harassment	☐	☐	☐
I am not recognised as a person in my own right	☐	☐	☐
My family commitments are seen as a liability	☐	☐	☐
I feel discriminated against	☐	☐	☐
I'm expected to work late to show commitment	☐	☐	☐
Out of hours fraternising is expected	☐	☐	☐
My partner and I clash about career priorities	☐	☐	☐
My working pattern causes serious problems	☐	☐	☐
I worry about redundancy/unemployment/ retirement	☐	☐	☐

4. WORKING SOLUTIONS

Don't feel daunted by the catalogue of problems in the previous chapter. There are ways to cope with them all, and starting to tackle them puts you in control - one of the best antidotes to stress.

Bear in mind that it is to your employer's advantage that you should feel happy and positive about work - it means that you will work better. So although you might fear raising awkward issues, they should be brought out in the open where they can be dealt with.

Employers need your skills. Replacing you costs money, time and administrative effort - and employers know that experienced people generally perform better, make fewer mistakes and need less supervisory time. In addition, you are a better, more coordinated, mature worker for being a working parent. If you can cope with toddler tantrums, you can cope with that irate customer. Employers appreciate this, and many are making efforts to accommodate parents. Here are a few examples of what some employers are prepared to do:

● a television company has introduced a system of childcare payments to staff of £120 a month, including pro-rata rates for part-timers: it considers job-share arrangements for all vacancies and it has increased the length of paid maternity and paternity leave. The key objectives are 'the retention and attraction of valuable skills and resources.'

● a local authority which is 80 per cent staffed by women offers a variety of part-time and flexible contracts. In addition, 12 per cent of women in the two most senior grades work non-traditional working patterns, which include working term-times only or job shares. As well as offering a wide range of permutations of flexitime, the authority has recently won an award for its range of flexiplace schemes, which allows employees to work from home as well as the office.

● a large multinational offers working mothers in senior management positions or with rare skills, the option of three career breaks of up to two years each, to a maximum of five years. They are allotted a mentor and asked to work for four weeks in each year to keep abreast of changes and developments. The same company also arranges for employees to work from home several days a week, where applicable, linked to the head office by computer and fax.

TACKLING PROBLEMS IN YOUR JOB

Where am I going?

Knowing where you are heading can help you develop a strategy for the future, and also to tolerate aspects of your job that are annoying if they are otherwise necessary stages towards a greater goal. On the other hand, having a vision of where you want to be can show you that you need to make more radical changes. Are you no longer as ambitious as you were, but still following the same career path? A change of work and pace might be the answer. On the other hand, do you now feel ready for a greater challenge than work offers? Perhaps you need to retrain and look for something more demanding.

Setting goals can be liberating and inspiring. It gives an outline and impetus to your working life. If you can see the wider picture, it can help you bear a routine job or one in which you are under-employed.

Set your goal Where do you envisage yourself professionally in a few years' time and what working pattern would suit you? Aim high by all means, but then outline the stages you need to get there. Can they realistically be achieved? If you want to wind down your responsibilities, can you target someone who could start to be trained to take over some of your work?

Remain flexible Don't be too rigid in setting your goals. It can take longer than you would like to reach a particular rung on the ladder, and feeling that you've failed if you don't get there as fast as you envisaged is unhelpful. Also your priorities can change: last year you wanted to be head of department; this year you discover that you value your less responsible role. If your job is more high-powered than you wish, could you make a sideways move, rather than off-loading some of your work?

Explore options Find other people who are doing what you want to do - or have done it, including people who wound down to a slower tempo if that is relevant. What steps did they take? If you want to change career it might be worth investing in professional advice (see chapter 8).

Organise your workload

Before you decide that there is something wrong with your job and the amount of work you have to do, it is worth seeing if you can organise your time more effectively.

List your priorities Work out which tasks you need to do now and which can wait. Pausing to take stock will help you stop approaching everything that crops up as a crisis.

Finish each task you start You probably know it yourself, but you will never feel in control if you don't clear that overflowing in-tray or work through that mental list of jobs half-done. Do one thing at a time and take steps to avoid being interrupted.

Pace yourself	Arrange short breaks during the day and turn off from work for a few minutes. Take time for lunch if you can. If possible, get away from your work place altogether. If not, don't continue working while you eat your sandwich. These short breaks are refreshing and you more than make up for the time later with increased energy.
Delegate where you can	You will have more time for the essential elements of your job if you can delegate. The classic excuse is that you can do it better than anyone - but if you don't give them the practice they won't learn.
Prepare for quieter periods	Hold back some non-urgent jobs until then. Use the time positively to bring everything right up to date.

If you are bored at the beginning of a new job, plan interesting things to do in the lunch hours; focus on your wider ambitions in the job.

'I came back from maternity leave to a hiatus and nothing to do. I wrote different CVs and tried actively to look for work outside. I wanted to do something constructive.'

Take control of timing	If you are in a position to influence the times of meetings, work out when you need to leave work, or the earliest time you can arrive, and only make yourself available between those times.

'I never fix meetings that start after 4pm: when people ask me when I'm available, I give a range of times, but never late afternoon.'

Don't specify what your other 'appointment' is if a school sports day or your child's dental check-up clashes with a suggested meeting. You need only say 'I'm busy then' before suggesting an alternative time.

'I knew that no one would acknowledge that I might want to get home at the end of the day to see my children. So I decided before I returned to work that I would make sure I left every day at 5.30pm. My office is full of people who stay late for the sake of it and because they think it looks good: I wanted to establish that I have a clear reason for leaving on time.'

A positive, assertive attitude is crucial in handling the expectation that you should work longer than your contracted hours. People who work efficiently should be able to do what is necessary in the time available. There is no particular merit in staying late or arriving at the crack of dawn.

'I need to do some client entertainment to keep the work coming in, but I do as little as I can. I would much rather be at home putting my children to bed. It hasn't hampered my prospects at work at all.'

Anticipate stress and prepare for it

Unexpected events cannot be prepared for, but you will be aware of situations that always cause you anxiety, such as regular meetings at which you must give a report. Plan ahead how you would like the event to go, decide in what way you should behave differently, and rehearse this. Decide also what to do if it doesn't go as well as you have hoped, and plan to give yourself a treat afterwards.

Overcoming practical problems

Many problems can be improved by quite straightforward changes. It may be a question of challenging the way you do things now and investigating alternatives.

The work environment

Talk to others in your department about changes that would improve the physical environment - your immediate boss might also be suffering and welcome practical suggestions. Could you move your desk, or bring in plants to make the atmosphere better? Could they install an ioniser to improve the air quality?

The journey to work

Could you change the hours you work to avoid rush hours? Could you change your route or the transport you use? Could you work at home? Could you turn the journey to the nursery into valuable time with your child in which you play games or talk about things you have no time for in the rush to get out of the house?

General worries

Some of the tensions looked at in the last chapter were of the 'what if?' category. The main way of dealing with these is to list your concerns, be they redundancy, unemployment, retirement or managing as a self employed person. Look at your list and see what practical solutions there are, if any. Make a timetable for dealing with them. Where there is nothing practical to be done, be firm about not letting yourself dwell on them. Worrying about the future in an unfocussed way is debilitating.

Intractable practical problems, and those to do with working conditions, colleagues or bosses, however, need a different approach. This involves brushing up your communication skills and finding the most effective way to reach a solution.

Developing your communication skills

Communicating well is one of the most vital workplace skills. It is how you make others aware of you, your views and needs. It includes skills such as being good on the telephone and effective in meetings. If you can communicate effectively, you are likely to find you have a greater sense of being in control. For example, if you are confident that you can talk problems through with others without becoming embroiled in a fight you can approach your job with more equanimity.

When you are unhappy about matters at work and there are changes that you want, you have to approach the subject in a way that gives you the best chance of success. To do so you must feel reasonably confident, present yourself assertively but pleasantly and 'play the game' - that is, bear in mind that you will get a better reception if you are able to demonstrate that what you are asking for benefits your employer as well as yourself.

Improving your self-esteem This involves realising your worth and learning to value yourself, both as a working person and a working parent. Low self-esteem often occurs amongst working mothers because of a sense of being unappreciated and undervalued. Similarly, fathers who are fully involved with their children and appreciated by their families can meet incomprehension, teasing or lack of respect at work because of this. A trainer who specialises in self-esteem workshops for employers, says: 'It is vital to recognise that you are valuable to yourself, your employers and your family; you are unique. You need to think about the qualities which make you so valuable and unique. It is important to consistently think well of and respect yourself. Colleagues will respond, and it will give you more confidence in dealing with people.'

Improving self-esteem involves re-evaluating your view of yourself and your worth. Make a list of the things you do well. Include qualities you have developed as a parent that enhance your value as an employee. You have matured: developed warmth, tolerance, endurance, a sense of responsibility, and so on - children teach you to expect the unexpected and cope with it. You have increased your ability to juggle a number of activities at once, while keeping an eye on an active child, ready to dart to the rescue or soothe. These are management skills. There are likely to be a number of other practical talents that have emerged: list them all.

When you learn to respect and value yourself more it becomes easier to respect others. Respect in this sense doesn't mean 'admire'. It means recognising that they too are people with value and feelings, who need to be treated with the care you would wish for yourself. It is always pleasanter to work where there is mutual respect. This includes trying to understand the people with whom you work. What pressures are they under that make them behave as they do? Acknowledging their difficulties as well as your own can help you find working solutions that suit you all.

Developing negotiating skills

The secret of negotiating well is to aim for a package that is acceptable to everyone. Work out what would be the best outcome for you and how far you are prepared to compromise from this position. Put yourself in the other person's shoes and assess what they are likely to prefer, and what they might give in on. Be firm and patient: patience is often the key to successful negotiation. The best outcomes often involve give on both sides. These essential elements of communication are just as useful at home - with older children and your partner. If you are troubled by conflicting priorities in your careers for example, it is more useful to reach for a compromise than to feel one of you must give in.

Becoming more assertive

Assertiveness is an essential life tool - especially in the workplace. If you work for a difficult boss, you won't be able to change his or her awkward nature - unfortunately! - but you may be able to restrict his or her impact on your job and prospects if you are confident you can cope.

Assertiveness can be developed with practice. It is about being confident and straightforward, which means standing up for your rights without violating the rights of others, and expressing yourself honestly and directly without feeling afraid or anxious. When you start becoming assertive, you stop feeling a victim or martyr. Assertiveness is also about assuming responsibility for yourself and how you use your own power.

To be reasonable and assertive you must curb your anger about things that often annoy you. This is best done by tackling minor annoyances before they have time to grow into major grievances. Another solution is to look for the funny side. When you are able to show humour as well as respect to others, it is likely to lessen bad feeling between you.

Learn to say no When you have too much to do, at home or at work, and this is making you feel angry and down, you should analyse how much of it you are bringing on yourself. Often the very things that overload us are the ones we have agreed to do in a weak moment. It is no good blaming someone else if you have said 'yes' when you should have said 'no'.

If you have difficulty saying no, start by giving yourself thinking time. When you are asked to take something on say, 'I'm not sure, I'll have to get back to you.' If you are pushed to give an instant answer, say 'I'm afraid I have to say no in that case. ' Take your time about analysing whether it is something you can realistically handle or not. If it is too much, say no. Or offer a compromise 'I could do that if I leave this other job until tomorrow, or someone else takes it over - which would you prefer?'

Once you have said no and meant it, don't waver or apologise, or you are likely to find yourself cajoled or nagged into changing your mind. Repeat yourself firmly and pleasantly: 'I'm too busy at the moment', 'I can't finish this and do that as well', 'That is not part of my job', or whatever is your reason.

For example, suppose your manager has asked you to attend a meeting on your day off. You want to say no, but you're not in the habit of doing so, these are the steps you should take:

● Ask for an appointment to discuss it with her. This gives you the chance to prepare and shows that the matter is serious for you. Identify exactly what the problem is: you took the job on the understanding that you didn't work Thursdays. You have no childcare arrangements on Thursday, and so on. Come up with a working compromise you could put forward, such as an alternative day. You should aim for something to offer rather than a stand off.

● Explain your reasons in a straightforward, unapologetic and reasonable way. Stick to your reasons in the discussion   and repeat them if necessary. Suggest the working compromise to show flexibility if it seems appropriate.

● Make sure you refute unreasonable or irrelevant points in a calm, logical way. Don't let yourself be manipulated, drawn into an argument or browbeaten by irrelevant facts. Aim to come away having said no to attending the meeting; having either arranged it for a different day, or agreed a compromise, such as someone standing in for you and filling you in afterwards.

You will find people respect you more when you show respect for your own time and work capacity.

'It has been hard learning to say no and I still find it difficult. I certainly didn't always feel so confident. But I know I am within my rights to say no to something if it means staying after the time I normally finish.'

Becoming more confident about your personal rights and when it is appropriate to say no is helpful in more awkward situations, such as harassment. In some cases fear of being disliked or of losing your job or of being thought prim can make you feel you should attempt to tolerate behaviour that would be better nipped in the bud immediately. A firm, pleasant, but unapologetic insistence that you will not put up with this will work in many cases.

Taking criticism Communicating well also means listening carefully. This involves learning how to take criticism. Constructive criticism is about helping you do what you do better, it is not an attack on you. These are the steps you should take:

● Acknowledge the criticism: 'I understand you wanted a more comprehensive report from me at the meeting'. You needn't apologise unless it is something you have been told before and know you have done wrong.

● Agree in principle: 'This is something I must take into account for next time'.

● Ask for clarification: 'Could you explain what you mean by "comprehensive" and tell me what I should have included?'

The point is to take it, but not lying down. You know you are not above criticism but you need to know more, and you are then willing to look at what needs to be changed.

Presenting a proposal

You need to use all these communication skills when you are presenting a proposal to your boss, your union, or to colleagues.

What needs to change? First you need to identify clearly which aspect of the job is causing you problems. Is it that you are being asked to do too much? Is it that you feel your talents aren't being put to the best use? Are you bothered by a colleague smoking?

When you have isolated the main problem, consider any sensible, practical and realistic changes that would make a difference. If you are underemployed, draw up proposals of ways to increase your workload that would benefit your employer. If you feel left out of office communications, you could ask to have your name added to the circulation list. Could your colleague smoke in a separate room or could you move? Practical solutions can have immediate effects.

Who can effect the change? Identify the person who can do something about it or find out if there is a policy or procedure you can follow. If you are bothered by a colleague smoking, a direct approach first is better than going over his or her head. Similarly, if you are being harassed your first move should be to tackle the harasser. However if you want a rise, it is less useful to complain to your boss's secretary, when it is your boss who makes the decision.

Preparing a proposal The aim is to show that you are being constructive, not just grumbling or making trouble. Have ready a clear, positive and realistic proposal, supported where relevant by facts and figures to back up your case.

If you are asking for a rise, a change in working conditions, or similar, find out if anyone else has successfully negotiated this. Talk to that person, who might have advice on strategy, or be able to give you facts to strengthen your own presentation. It will also demonstrate that you have done your homework.

Prepare to negotiate. Ask for the best outcome from your point of view, but have in mind the essential points on which you are determined to stand firm and others that you are willing to concede.

If you are making a complaint, the procedure is similar. For instance, if you are being harassed, a list of what your harasser has done, with dates and examples, as well as how you have tried to contain the situation yourself, will be taken more seriously than a tearful outburst about how difficult your life has been made.

Practise your proposal

Ask your partner or a friend to listen to your proposal. Let them pick holes in your presentation - and listen to what they say. It can help to anticipate the questions or objections you might face, and prepare answers. Ask your partner or friend to play devil's advocate and give you a hard time. Practise until you are happy with what you plan to say.

Arrange the meeting

Make an appointment to see whoever you have identified - line manager, boss and so on - or send a memo. You need to decide which method is likely to be the most effective. It might be more appropriate to ask for a pay rise face to face; if you are putting forward ideas to make your job more interesting, you may want to put suggestions down on paper. As a general rule, it is a good idea to have everything in writing even if you are going to talk about it, and memos are more likely to be read and understood if you explain them too.

Suppose, for example, that you are frustrated because you are not being given the responsibility you were promised when you took on the job. Work out which tasks you think you could take on; what qualities you could bring to those responsibilities, and calculate how you would fit them into your work schedule. Itemise the advantages there would be for your employer and present all these points as a package - making sure to leave room for manoeuvre and compromise.

Similarly, if you are being asked to do too much, you need to clarify your areas of responsibility. If you are over-stretched, explain exactly what you can cope with and what is proving too much for you. Work out a list of priorities and present a time plan. Make it clear that you have thought it through and want to find a constructive solution. Say that it is not that you are unwilling, but that the amount of pressure means that you are not able to devote the time to the crucial parts of your job you think they need. It is best to be honest but unapologetic.

Case study

Kate had returned full-time to her job as a senior secretary in a hospital after her first child was born. However, after the birth of her second child she was reluctant to work 9 to 5; apart from wanting more time with her children, her older child was not settling down well in nursery school because of the changes at home.

She did not feel there was anything she could do about this apart from leave, until she joined her local working parents group. 'Your employer may value your skills and knowledge of how the hospital ticks more than you imagine' was the advice she received. 'Plan a meeting with your boss and show that you have thought through the implications of the change, both the benefits to you and how the organisation could deal with your absence.'

Kate was pleasantly surprised to find that her employer was indeed prepared to negotiate rather than lose her altogether, and she was able to arrange to work a shorter day, arriving at 8.30 and finishing at 3pm. 'I sometimes have to take work home to look over in the evenings, but I am always able to collect my daughter from nursery school. She has settled down well and I enjoy having more energy for the end of the day and bathtime with the baby.'

After presenting your proposal You may not immediately get the response you want. You may have planted ideas that need careful consideration. You may be asked to supply additional information, or you might be asked to concede more than you had originally planned. Keep calm and take time yourself to come up with further answers or consider whether you are prepared to compromise further.

Dealing with 'no' If you are reasonable and have presented a well-considered proposal you are most likely to find that all or some of your demands are acceptable. But you should also prepare for the fact that they might be turned down. Are you prepared to go to a higher authority or to leave? Don't threaten anything you are unwilling to carry out. If you back down and yet nothing has changed, you will be even less happy than before.

Changing corporate culture

Dealing with unfriendly working practices can make you feel you are up against something very big. You might be - but on the other hand it could be the case that no one has questioned the traditions before. Rather than feel outraged and combative, therefore, you should look at what needs changing, and follow the steps for presenting a proposal. It is only if this fails that you need to think more radically. In this case you could consider joining a lobbying organisation or a workplace action group, if one exists, or setting one up.

Setting up a working parents group

Contact other working parents in your organisation or send round a memo to see if anyone is interested. Fix a preparatory meeting at which you can discuss what the group's aims should be and how often it should meet.

It is worth varying the days and location of meetings so that everyone has a chance to attend. Fix a number of dates in advance, perhaps with themes or topics. An aspect working parents appreciate is the chance to get together to share and discuss experiences, but you may also find it helpful to decide on some concrete aims. These might include liaison with management over the needs of working parents; a contact point for employees on maternity leave and support for working mothers returning to work.

With such a group, you can support each other when it comes to asking for changes and putting forward proposals.

Changing working patterns

Changing the hours you work can be the single most helpful move you make. If you feel pressured because you are not spending as much time with your children as you would like, flexible working patterns might suit you.

Flexitime and part-time

Flexitime means being able to arrange your own working hours within a given framework. It is one of the most attractive options for parents, as is working part-time, financial drawbacks notwithstanding.

44

'I work a four day week, with Wednesdays off,' says a PR executive with two children. 'On that day I do the shopping and sort out all our arrangements for the week. It means the weekends are mostly free of chores. I don't get paid as much as if I worked five days of course, which is a drawback, but I don't think I could manage without that extra day.'

Case study

Jennifer worked in a chemist's shop but had given up work when her daughter was young after splitting up with her partner. 'The cost of childcare was too high for me on my own and I wanted to spend more time with Janine after her dad left.' When Janine started school, Jennifer thought about returning to work but was concened about holiday care. 'There was a playscheme at the local school but I felt Janine was too young to go to it full-time.' When she approached her former employer about returning to work at their local branch she was interested to find out that it would be possible for her to have a term-time only contract.

'I had a good work record with the company and they were pleased to have me back for their new superstore. They recruit local students to work in the holidays to cover when term-time-only workers are not there. The students benefit from the work experience and I don't have to worry about Janine in the holidays. When she is a little older she may be ready for the playscheme and I might extend my hours then.'

If you have identified that discrimination arising from working part-time is undermining your satisfaction, deal with this by looking at best practice examples from other employers, and check out the legal position. Present a proposal incorporating these points, and look for support from colleagues in the same position. If you can't effect change, remember why you are working part-time and enjoy the flexibility it gives you: keep a positive attitude.

'I don't consider my jobs part-time,' says a mother of two and a manager in an information technology department, 'It's just that they let me work three days instead of five. All my conditions, including my pension are worked out on a pro rata basis for a full-time salary so I don't feel disadvantaged at all. I do it because I really value the time at home and the chance to go to mother and toddler groups.'

45

Job-share You have the benefits of doing an interesting job at the right level for you, and still manage to spend a good deal of time with your children.

'It's the best thing that's ever happened to me,' says a mother of one who job-shares in a television programme finance department. 'I can be a mother and a working person, I don't have to compromise either. I'm at the same level as before my maternity leave, I get to share the responsibility of the job with someone else and it is fun if you can work well together. My sharer and I have become close friends. I get three fifths of the salary and work a three day week. On the day my sharer and I overlap, we have meetings with commissioning editors. Nothing has to be discussed twice.'

Case study

Sylvia and her husband Patrick are both librarians working in a large London reference library. When their son was born they both wanted to spend time with him and equally wished to maintain their careers. As they both work for the same employer and have similar skills, a job-share seemed the ideal solution.

'A suitable vacancy arose for which we could make a case for a job-share while Sylvia was on maternity leave, so I asked personnel to consider us for the post. The library did not have any job-shares at the time but I was able to give an example of a neighbouring borough library with a successful job-sharing scheme to reassure them. The only snag was that I am on a lower grade than Sylvia and she had to accept a reduction in her salary to share the post. However, the benefits to us all are enormous in terms of a family - and we've saved on childcare costs which help offset the loss of income.' Sylvia points out that the library has benefited too: 'We liaise at home over hand-over work in the library and they've got two sets of brains for the price of one!'

Flexiplace schemes The advent of home links to computer networks, cheap fax machines and electronic mail services has made it possible for many people to work from home, or to combine working from home with one or two days a week at the office.

Case study

Julie, a mother of three is a speech writer for the managing directors of a large multinational company and works a four day week, three at home and one at the central London headquarters.

'I see a lot of the children with this arrangement. I almost always have lunch with them and can even take them to the park. Because I don't have to travel into work, my hours away from them are not as long as they would otherwise be. I spend one day in the London office having meetings with the people I'm writing for. I'm not so well off financially - I only get London weighting for the day I go into the office, but I feel extremely fortunate with this arrangement.'

Career breaks

These can be of varying lengths, and you may be able to take several during the course of your career. Though you are unlikely to be able to return to exactly the same job, the arrangement is usually that you should return to a job of similar status.

Working from home

If working at home, either for an employer or for yourself, results in you feeling isolated, take steps to combat this. Arrange to have lunch with your children or a friend on a regular basis. Build up contacts and support networks. Pick up the phone and talk to people. If you have someone in the house looking after the children while you are working, fix a timetable so that you know when the house will be quiet and when you can move about in it as you please.

'It has been a big transition, and at first I didn't feel I belonged anywhere, either at home or work. It takes time to meet people but I am gradually getting to know some people through my son's school. I really appreciate having more than an hour a day with my children which was all I had before. I am starting to thoroughly enjoy it.'

If none of these options is on offer to you, you may have to suggest them yourself. It could be that your employers simply haven't thought about it, not that they are against any of them. Offering flexible working is one of the cheapest and easiest to implement of family friendly policies.

CHECKLIST

*Look at the difficulties you isolated in the TROUBLESHOOTER
checklist at the end of the last chapter. Take a separate sheet
of paper for each and answer the following questions:*

1. *What needs to change to make this better?*

   List all possible changes separately.

2. *Who can make these changes?*

   *Mark the ones you can do yourself, and those which need
   to be carried out by someone else.*

3. *My changes.*

   *List the steps you need to take to make changes yourself,
   and then give yourself a timetable for making them.*

4. *What I want someone else to do.*

   *Look at what you are asking and, putting yourself in that
   person's shoes, list all the possible objections you can
   imagine the person making.*

5. *My answers.*

   *Look at the objections and consider how you will deal with
   them. Do you need extra information to back up your
   argument? Where will you get it?*

5. DEMANDS AT HOME

One of the best antidotes to stress is a change of focus. When your mind has been running on a particular problem, switching off from it and becoming involved in something new can be refreshing. Family life, therefore, puts work in perspective. For this reason, working parents often find that full and demanding evenings and weekends with the family paradoxically relieve work-related stress. Even workaholics have to turn their thoughts away from their job when a child wants to have a cuddle or play a game, or a partner has something to discuss, or one of the hundred and one practical issues to do with living as a family crops up. Many working parents cite this as the reason they believe they work more efficiently than they did when work considerations occupied all their thinking time.

Nevertheless it is difficult to combine these two major areas of life without hitting the occasional crisis. When everyone is well and happy and arrangements are working smoothly it's fine. But if the baby cries all night, the school closes for a day without warning, the washing machine packs up and you have to wait in for the engineer - or there is any other major or minor hiccup - panic rises, your temper frays and once again you feel under pressure.

This chapter looks at the areas of home and family life that can go wrong at times. Again, it would be rare indeed for everything to coincide at once; and, on the bright side, dealing with a crisis successfully can make you feel strong and in control.

The purpose is to help you pinpoint any issue that is constantly on your mind and therefore undermining you more than it should. This is what you need to tackle urgently, and the next chapter offers ideas. This chapter also helps alert you to the one-off emergency that can give you problems. Forewarned is forearmed and again, in the next chapter, you will find measures to help you create a safety net.

NEW BABY

If this is your first baby, you will probably be experiencing new and confusing emotions. Along with these will come anxieties about balancing work demands with the needs of your baby and, perhaps, your partner. With a second baby, there may be additional concerns, for instance about how your older child will take to a sibling and how you are going to meet all the needs of your growing family.

Pregnancy

You may feel vulnerable and take criticism more personally than you would under other circumstances. You may feel more dependent on your partner. Whether it is a first, or subsequent pregnancy, you will feel tired. Tasks you whipped through before can now seem burdensome chores.

'The baby was born just after Christmas, and when she was four weeks old my childcare fell through. Later that week, my husband fell ill and was off work for a week. In the meantime I was having to cope with my son's intense feelings of anger and jealousy. We survived. Now, four months on, many of those problems seem just a faint memory.'

Parenthood

As a new parent, you may feel torn between spending time with your family and working to sustain the family income. Trying to be all things to everyone can leave you with feelings of confusion over your divided loyalties and a sense that you can't please anyone .....

CHILDCARE

Working parents in the throes of making childcare arrangements name it as their biggest worry. Thankfully, once the arrangements are up and running it becomes, like everything, routine, and is only bothersome when things go wrong.

'The availability of a reliable source of childcare is my biggest source of stress,' says a personnel officer and mother of one who lives in Cumbria. 'Registered childminders are very few and far between.'

Choosing your childcare

When choosing your childcare you need to select the option with which you feel most comfortable, and which fits in with your budget, commitments, and ages and needs of your children. Whether this is a relative, childminder, nursery, nanny, au pair, out-of-school scheme or mixture of more than one, there are good points and drawbacks to each. The Working Parents Handbook helps you make this decision.

When your choice is a good match with your needs you are likely to feel relaxed about it. However there are certain issues that can result in this being an area of tension for you.

Problems with timing

The hours of the childcarer don't fit well with your work commitments. There is a rush at either end of the day or your lateness creates difficulties.

The carer's approach

You are not convinced that your children are being looked after the way you would wish, perhaps in terms of attention, discipline, stimulation or the food they are given, although outwardly all seems fine.

Children unhappy

They appear reluctant to be left and show disruptive behaviour at other times.

Difficulties arranging care

This is most likely with school-age children, who finish in the early afternoon and have long holidays, but is also possible with younger children if your arrangements are not permanent.

51

'I had an awful performance with the first nanny. She was late almost every morning. I would feel as though I'd done a whole day's work by the time I got there. We quickly changed to someone who lives in.'

The emotional conflict

Many childcare arrangements work excellently and happily, but some are affected by the conflicting emotions that are stirred up when you employ someone to care for your child. People who make competent managers at work can still find it difficult to have a similar professional relationship with a carer.

You may feel jealous if the children develop attachments to the carer, even though it is best for them that they should. You may feel guilty about not staying home with your children yourself.

'I've had good experiences with nannies so far, but with the present one I have quite a few emotional problems. Demarcation is a very difficult area. Sometimes my children come in and run to her and I feel jealous.'

Temporary upheavals

Usually childcare arrangements run smoothly after the settling-in period. But there will be the odd occasion when they break down: the childminder's holiday doesn't coincide with yours, the nursery won't take your child because he is infectious, granny is ill and so on. These times are stressful but they do pass, and are tests of your contingency arrangements (see next chapter).

Finding a new carer

There can come a time when you need to change your childcare, either because you are not happy with it, or because your child's needs have changed, or because your childcarer has given notice. It takes time and effort to visit or interview for a new option. Your routine will change, and you have to settle the children again.

Selecting schools

While schools are not, of course, childcare options, choosing the right one for your child can be as time-consuming as looking for childcare for younger children, particularly at secondary level. Visiting times can be inflexible, and it can mean taking a number of days off work.

Settling your child into primary school

You might want or need to arrange to be around more when your children first start school, which puts pressure on work commitments.

FAMILY DYNAMICS

Having a family gives you stability and a reason for doing what you do - whether it is just you and one child, or you are married with several children. But family life, enjoyable and enriching as it is, makes its own demands. When things go wrong for the people you love, or when your relationships with them run into difficulties, the stress can be greater than the worst upheaval at work.

This is when the dual nature of the working parent's life can again come to the rescue. Work can seem a piece of cake when home is in chaos - and many parents report that work saved their sanity when their children were going through a difficult patch, or during a divorce.

There are usually two high tension points in each day. One is the early morning dash to get everyone and assorted school bags, sports bags and briefcases out of the door by 8am; the other is the evening rush, the hours between 6pm and 8pm when everyone is tired and trying to grab supper, watch television, do homework, make an important phone call, have a bath and get the children to bed. A similar scenario will be familiar to you.

Problems with children

Coping with babies and young children

Adjusting to a new baby, whether it is your first or your fourth, is demanding, particularly when you are in paid work too. You are tired, and you have to learn about the unique needs of the new arrival in your household.

Older children may feel jealous of a new baby. The existing family will have to adapt to different family dynamics. You may have to change your childcare arrangements now that the family is a different size.

You may have a child at a difficult age, or you may find all ages difficult! Children have problems at times: eating and sleeping; going to bed and getting up in the morning; waking up with nightmares and so on. One moment your children may be playing happily, the next moment fighting.

Coping with teenagers

Your delightful son may become bolshy overnight; nothing you can say or do is right for your daughter. You may feel rejected or always on the verge of an argument.

Even when your relationship with your children is very good, they will have ups and downs of their own anyway. You are alert to their feelings however old they are. If they are going through a bad patch with friends or at school it is difficult not to worry about it yourself.

Children with special needs or disabilities

This is of course a subject for a separate book and you will be well aware of what it means to your lives and the additional pressures it brings to home and work.

'My son has cerebral palsy; it was a late diagnosis and so there has been a long series of on-going assessments. There are a lot of appointments to attend with specialists. We used to have a lot of therapists calling at the house, and we have to maintain contact with the specialists and coordinate all the treatments and appraisals. Having been able to take advantage of a flexible workplace scheme and do a lot of my work from home has helped enormously.'

Problems with your partner

Not all partners are supportive and, sadly, not all supportive partners are as helpful as they think they are. If there is no clear understanding of who does what it can create continuing conflict.

Conflicts are a fact of life and a feature of relationships. If they escalate, however, this can overshadow other areas of your life - children and work included. Marital breakdown is at the top of the scale of life incidents that cause stress. If divorce is the result there is a period of emotional upheaval for you and your children, as well as practical and financial problems. These problems are similar but intensified for people whose partners die.

'We don't live near any relatives so I have no one I can easily call on. If I forget something like a loaf of bread, I have to get both children dressed to go out and get one. I don't let them get as dirty and dishevelled as other children if we are out having fun, because I know when we get home it is me who has to undress them, cope with the muddy boots and do all the washing. There is no one else.'

A carer to everyone

You envy the working parent who has just one child, a supportive partner and no elderly relatives to care for. Your partner, whom you love, nevertheless expects you to do everything. Your children are adorable but demanding. Your mother is ill and needs visiting regularly. As if that weren't enough, your friends, when you finally take an evening off to go out with them, take this opportunity to unburden themselves of their troubles. You are so understanding. You are however, also about to scream...

THE HOME ROUTINE

With luck your home is your castle: you feel safe, comfortable and relaxed. But it needs looking after, which takes time and money. Family routines - even the pleasureable ones - need planning. It is an added pressure if money is tight and your living conditions are less than ideal.

Housework Few people enjoy housework, but it is has to be done. It can be a source of argument between you and your partner - one of you is clean and tidy and the other isn't.

The demands of school You feel concerned about the quality of your children's schooling. Once children start having homework and taking important exams you feel the need to become involved in this too. They may have a number of hobbies and extra-curricular activities to attend and have to be taken and collected.

'I need to invest a lot of time, both at the beginning of the day getting ready for school and at the end, sorting tomorrow's things and encouraging homework. Life seems an endless round of filling school bags with packed lunches and school books and emptying out the manky old gym kit.'

CRISES AND TIME-CONSUMING EVENTS

These are the occasions when the smooth running of your daily life is likely to be disrupted for a time.

One offs and annual events Talk to any working parent who's just given a birthday party for the five year old, and you will have a clear picture of stress!

Other occasions include trips to the dentist or doctor that conflict with working hours; having to contribute to school events; your parents, in-laws or any guests to stay; Christmas and its demands; and the annual holiday.

Illness   This causes difficulties whether it is you, your children or your childcarer.

> 'The worst day for me was when my partner and I had gastro-enteritis. We were both self employed and working from home with no childcare, so we took it in turns to have half an hour in bed, while the other one looked after our two year old son.'

In the next chapter there are positive ideas and suggestions for making home life and occasional problems such as these run more smoothly.

SNAPPING POINTS

Which aspects of your home and family life need addressing? Look at the statements on this chart and give yourself 0 if it is not a problem; 1 if it bothers you intermittently; and 2 if it is affecting your ability to cope. The ones on which you score 2 are those you need to tackle first.

	0	1	2
I'm pregnant and finding it harder to cope	☐	☐	☐
I'm not happy about my childcare arrangements	☐	☐	☐
I think my child is too attached to the carer	☐	☐	☐
I worry that it is wrong for someone else to look after my child	☐	☐	☐
My children seem fine now, but I worry they might not be	☐	☐	☐
My children seem unhappy	☐	☐	☐
I am having difficulties with my children	☐	☐	☐
I don't spend enough time with my partner	☐	☐	☐
I am not getting on with my partner	☐	☐	☐
Bringing my children up on my own is a problem	☐	☐	☐
Everyone expects me to look after them - yet no one looks after me	☐	☐	☐
Housework gets me down	☐	☐	☐
Monitoring my children's schooling is worrying and time-consuming	☐	☐	☐
I don't know how I would manage if my childcare arrangements broke down or my children were ill	☐	☐	☐
I never know what to say at work if I have to take time off for home commitments	☐	☐	☐

6. DEALING WITH HOME LIFE

The last chapter showed some of the difficult phases life at home can go through. A closer examination reveals that the problems fall into a small number of categories.

The first to tackle is the 'what if...' worry. This is the guilt-driven, imagination-powered worry that has no real basis in what is happening now, but which is easily activated simply because you are loving and concerned. Worrying about your children when there is no current problem is an example of this. These worries are debilitating precisely because they are unfocussed, and because there is no action you can usefully take. By allowing these worries to fill your mind, it is harder to cope with the real problems when they arise. Looking back to Chapter 2 can help with this.

Alongside learning how to consign these concerns to the background, you must deal with things that you can tackle. The most important is long-term stress: anything that is with you day to day or that may last longer than a year, such as coping with divorce. Can you do anything practical to make things easier for yourself? If so, do so. Whatever the problem, the key to making it bearable is to be ruthless about pruning non-essentials that add to your worries. If you have explored all possible avenues and come up against a dead-end, training yourself to relax, changing your focus, or one of the other methods mentioned in Chapter 2 will help. It is not self-indulgence, just sanity-saving sense.

The last category is the short-term problem, crisis, unusual or time-consuming event that temporarily makes things difficult for you. Firstly, take a long-term view - your common sense tells you it won't last forever. Secondly, be kind to yourself: remind yourself that it is wearing and do all you can to make things easier in other areas of your life. This includes explaining the problem to others - employers and friends - and asking for time, tolerance and help over this period. You might be surprised how co-operative people are when you are clear about the problem, its likely duration, and what you need from them. Thirdly, turn your attention to tackling the problem in the best way that you can. Action, in all cases, is better than nail-biting paralysis.

Some of the difficulties have specific solutions, and some of them are suggested here.

NEW BABY

Pregnancy

This is the classic be-kind-to-yourself time, and possibly the time you will find that others share your concerns and make allowances for you. Take advantage of it! Be forward about asking for help in sharing the tasks you now find difficult. Pushing yourself too hard serves no purpose.

It is difficult to predict how well you will feel during pregnancy, so it is best not to be too rigid in your time planning. You may have to stop work earlier than you thought; you may have to go to bed earlier than usual.

Don't make comparisons with previous pregnancies or with how other people cope: each pregnancy is unique. Allow yourself flexibility within the legal limits when fixing your return to work date.

Parenthood

Take as much time as possible from work to allow yourself to settle into your new routine and get to know your baby. See if your company is prepared to be more flexible about your working hours in the early months. Some employers may be willing to discuss a 'phased' return to work for new mothers. In addition to statutory employment rights, find out if you or your partner's workplace offer any family-friendly benefits, such as parental leave.

CHILDCARE

Choosing childcare

The more time you can give yourself to look at the various options the more relaxed you will feel. If you are working as you do so you will then be better able to space interviews and appointments so that they fit in with your work commitments.

Emotional conflict

Parents need time to adjust to being away from their children, just as children have to settle in to the new arrangement. Part of the adjustment can mean coping with guilty feelings until you see how well your children have adapted. If the feelings persist, however, you need to look objectively at why you are feeling guilty, and see if you can change anything to make yourself feel better. Often your guilt is groundless: your children are happy and thriving. If, however, they are not doing so well, or you miss spending more time with them, you might need to consider changing your working patterns (see Chapter 4), or your form of childcare (see below).

Guilt that is unspecific, however, and that you continue to feel despite your children's well-being, is in the category of self-induced stress. You owe it to yourself to concentrate on all the positive and good things you are doing for children and at work. It is too easy to forget them - and people who feel guilty are often the most conscientious.

Many working mothers feel guilty about leaving their children, particularly when they are very young. Yet increasingly the research in this area shows that the impact on children of having two working parents can be a positive one. Having a working mother can provide an excellent role model for girls and give them the opportunity to envisage wider possibilities for themselves; boys are likely to grow up with more understanding of sharing all aspects of family life.

Recognising that making mistakes is human is also important. As long as you do your best at work, and love, respect and care for your children, the odd mistake can be accepted with good humour and tolerance.

Worrying about your child's attachment to the carer is usually a by-product of guilt. Children need to love the adults who care for them, and it is healthier than merely tolerating or disliking them. It is a sign that they are happy with the arrangements. Remember that a child's capacity to love is not finite: you will not be loved less simply because someone else is loved too. Quite the reverse is true.

Problems with timing
When there is friction at the beginning and end of the day because childcaring hours and work hours conflict, you should look at a range of options. If your childcarer is an individual - childminder, nanny, au pair or relative - can you build in an agreement about hours when you need the care to start extra early or finish late? The simplest solution is to offer overtime calculated at a higher

rate. Remember also that in some cases it is the uncertainty that causes bad feeling. The courtesy of a warning when there might be a problem, or a phonecall if one crops up suddenly, with information about how long you expect to be, can make a difference.

If there is no flexibility of childcare - your child attends a nursery, out-of-school scheme, must be collected from school at a certain time, or your childcarer has other commitments which make it impossible - then one possibility is to change to a form of childcare that offers the flexibility you need. If you are reluctant to do this because you don't want to move your child and are otherwise happy, can you make a 'top-up' arrangement - that is, someone who is prepared to stand in for you during the crucial hours, whom you could pay or repay in some other way?

If none of these alternatives is possible or acceptable to you, then you need to look at re-arranging your work hours to solve the problem. Chapters 3 and 4 help you decide how to do this.

Worries about your childcarer's approach

It would be a miracle if you found someone whose approach was identical to your own, and most parents are prepared to be relatively tolerant so long as their children are happy, well-looked after and safe. Real concerns, however, should not be ignored but addressed as quickly as possible.

If your child is looked after at a nursery, out-of-school scheme or any arrangement where there is a generalised policy on care, it will be that much harder to impose your own ideas. Unless you are able to effect changes fairly quickly, you might decide it would be better to look for an alternative method of care for your child if it doesn't meet your standards.

When an individual is involved, however, you are in a much better position to make sure your own approach is followed within reasonable limits. With a childminder, nanny, au pair or relative it is best to set clear guidelines right from the start. It is helpful to write these down, and to cover everything that is important to you, such as feeding, discipline, play and general activities. If appropriate, set it out in a written contract. In this way there can be no misunderstandings about what you expect, and the carer can raise points over which there might be difficulties. It helps all concerned if your relationship is professional.

'I now write out very detailed contracts, right down to nail cutting and hair washing. She can't be expected to read my mind, yet it's the little things that add up and cause problems.'

Of course, some points might not occur to you at the beginning: perhaps as your child grows older new aspects occur to you, or it is only when your childcarer does something which disturbs you that you realise that you think differently.

These points should be raised quickly and directly. If you want your child to take a nap in the afternoon, tell the carer this. A hint such as 'John always seems so tired at the end of the day' is unhelpful: the carer doesn't know what you want but you feel annoyed because you think you have been tactful and your wishes are being ignored. It can also be useful to follow up with an informal letter detailing what your concerns are and what you believe has been agreed.

Once you have established the rules, try not to interfere or change them except when really necessary. If you do find yourself chopping and changing a lot ask yourself whether it is really necessary or whether it is perhaps connected to guilty feelings about not being with your children and a need to feel involved in the small details of their lives. If you can admit to yourself that this is the case you must recognise that it is not good for your children to be in the middle of conflicting adults. A carer who is exasperated with you is not ideal.

Conflicts with your carer

If you are having problems with your carer it will help if you can make time to talk without interruption from the children: misunderstandings can be cleared up during a good chat. As well as putting over your own point of view, ask her what she finds difficult and would like to change. Respect her as a fellow working woman and treat her as you would like an employer to treat you. This is more helpful even than making a friend of her - it is awkward telling a friend what to do, but is expected in a professional relationship.

'It's vital to be nice to your nanny. Allow time each week to sit down together for twenty minutes or so. Look at her photographs, listen to her and make her feel wanted.'

You may find other ways of making your childminder or nanny feel appreciated and wanted, such as buying flowers. It may seem obvious, but it will always help to say thank you if she has done something extra or you are especially pleased with your child's progress.

Your children are unhappy/ playing up

If your childcare arrangements continue to disturb you, or disturb your child, then you should not hesitate to change them. This is particularly the case if your child seems unhappy and reluctant to be left with the carer or, more importantly, shows disturbed and unhappy behaviour at other times. You need to distinguish between normal settling-in difficulties, when your child adjusts to being left, and longer term problems. Many children make a fuss when you leave them, even though they are otherwise quite contented with the carer. Usually, if your child seems happy at other times, and is no more than normally clingy there is probably little to worry about. But unusual clinginess, sadness or disruptive behaviour at other times, 'tummy aches' and other unspecific symptoms, and perhaps disturbed nights and nightmares will mean that you want to look closely at all aspects of your child's life, including care.

Talk to your carer to see if she can throw light on what is going on - there might be a perfectly legitimate explanation: your child was frightened by an encounter with a dog in the park, or is adjusting to a new child at the childminder's. Use your instinct as well as your commonsense to assess what she says. Take opportunities to spend time watching how your children and carer interact, perhaps arriving early or unexpectedly.

Changing to another carer whom you and your children prefer, although disruptive in the short-term, will ease your mind for the future.

Finding a new carer

Choosing childcare first, second or third time round, comes into the category of short-term stress. Yes, it's going to be time-consuming and worrying, but you will get there in the end. Explain calmly to your employer why you might need to be flexible during this period, but that it is finite.

Losing a carer you wanted to keep may be sad, but a new carer may bring other advantages and unexpected joys. She may have new skills, introduce a different perspective or get on better with a child who was second favourite with the last carer.

Be prepared for some hiccups in the early stages, and reserve your judgment until the new arrangement has been in place for at least two weeks, but then deal immediately with any concerns rather than letting them fester.

Choosing schools

Similar to choosing childcare, although your options are likely to be more restricted. You should let your employer know in the same way. School visiting times can be inflexible, and are usually bang in the middle of a working day. If you foresee difficulties, take holiday leave. Remember that you might want to revisit certain schools before making your final choice, so over-estimate the time it will take. It can help to talk to other parents whose children are at the schools you are considering (and you can do this in your own time). Ask the schools for names if you don't know any personally. As with anything to do with your children, you will be concerned and perhaps worried. Prepare for this by recognising the pressure and not over-loading yourself unecessarily during this time.

Settling your children into primary school

There are several ways in which you can prepare yourself and your children on a practical level. Make dry runs of the new journey and new routine. Pick up tips from other mothers about the new school and teachers to pass onto your children. You can read stories about starting school which will bring it to life and make those first days not so daunting.

Some children settle in instantly and with great enthusiasm, but others need more of your support and attention than usual. If your child is finding the transition difficult, you might want to consider taking some of your holiday at this time.

Temporary upheavals

What to do if your children are sick, or your childcare breaks down is something you need to address before it happens. It will be less difficult if you plan for it before it happens (see Getting Support, below).

Continuing difficulties arranging care

Where possible you should make arrangements that last for a decent length of time, even if it costs you more. What you save in terms of wear and tear on your nerves makes it worthwhile. With out-of-school care, this might mean engaging a childminder, or paying a friend or relative to take on the responsibility rather than relying on good-will and changes in availability. Some go-ahead people involve themselves in setting up their own out-of-school scheme (see Chapter 8 for organisations to help).

Case study

Shirley, a personnel manager in a large civil service office, discovered that many parents (herself included) found it difficult to organise good, reliable holiday care for school-age children. She carried out a survey of childcare needs in the office and age ranges of employees' children, which highlighted the lack of local provision and showed that a high proportion of parents had children at school. Using the evidence from the report, Shirley convinced her personnel director and finance department that it would be practical to run a summer play scheme for employees' children using a local private school shut for the holidays as a base for it. Administration time to plan the scheme and organise bookings was given free by the department, who also guaranteed the play scheme staff wages. The cost of running the scheme was met through a daily charge to parents using it. Shirley found that in the first year the scheme ran at a loss as places were not filled every day. But the second year she made sure the scheme was well publicised early in the year when parents were planning their summer holiday arrangements and it was fully booked. The scheme, now in its third year, has become well established and Shirley has solved her own childcare problems as her two children use it too.

FAMILY RELATIONSHIPS

As a working parent you might need reminding that family relationships go through difficult patches for everyone, working or not. This bears repeating because the burden is increased when guilt is added to the other feelings.

You don't need telling to make time for your children and your partner, it is probably what you try to do anyway. But so often working parents report that other commitments or chores get in the way. What you may need to do is remind yourself of your own priorities.

Be ruthless about the things you think you ought to do, but which give you less satisfaction. Are you doing housework to your mother's standards, or your mother-in-law's - when both of them were at home all day? Question whether this is necessary to you and whether you can have a less perfect home but more time for the family.

Don't take everything on yourself. When both of you are out at work it is only fair that you should share the chores and the parenting. Being part of a working couple is all about sharing responsibilities.

Time for your children

Children of different ages need different degrees of attention from you. The baby might want to be walked or to play the same game over and over; the schoolchild might want you to listen and laugh at inane jokes; an intense adolescent might want to talk about death or sex at 11.30 at night. Sometimes you might be in the mood, at others you are too tired or irritable and can't be bothered. They need your attention, of course. They need to feel loved and respected, and you need their feedback too. But there is no point in pushing yourself to the limit every time.

Sometimes you will have to find extra resources in yourself when one child is particularly needy, but there will also be occasions when it is perfectly fine to reschedule: 'I'll do that with you after supper' or 'I can't today, but tomorrow is my day off and we'll do it then'. You can also suggest alternatives: 'My eyes are tired, let me tell you a story instead' or 'Playing dinosaurs is too noisy, let's listen to your favourite songs'. If a number of children are competing for your attention you can build in exclusive time for each within your routine. You take one child with you to do the shopping or to help with a chore, or stagger their bed times so they have you to themselves. Time spent with a child doesn't have to be educational or memorable, just normal; it's special enough to feel loved, accepted and interesting.

If one of your children is going through a difficult time, regard this as a short-term problem, and deal with it accordingly. It won't last forever, but you might need extra help. If you don't have a partner to share the load, enlist family and friends to give yourself more time.

Time with your partner

Working couples who have sorted this one out say that there is only one real solution: get out your diaries, make dates and times and stick to them. Make sure that at least one of these per week is out of the house: either hire a babysitter or make arrangements with other couples to take turns to have your children to stay. What you do doesn't have to be expensive; you can nurse one drink in the pub or go for a walk if the weather is fine. Remind yourself that keeping your relationship in good shape benefits all the family - and is likely to be good for work too. Don't allow your bedroom to become the family room - make it an invitation-only treat once your children are no longer babies. A lock on the bedroom door is the cheapest and most effective sex accessory.

If your relationship is running into problems because you clash about division of responsibility or more fundamental issues such as disagreements about how to bring up your children, sorting it out will be top of your priorities. Time alone to do so is even more essential and you might consider counselling.

Divorce and becoming a single parent

This is one of the most stressful life events of all and as such you should treat it with the seriousness it deserves. To pull yourself through, you need all the help you can get: inform your employer and accept help from whatever quarter it comes. Helping yourself means cutting out as much as possible that adds to the stress, and rewarding yourself with treats and treatments that appeal to you.

A carer to everyone

While it is harder to say no to people you care for than it is to colleagues, it is just as essential if you are not going to be pulled in too many directions. Look back at Developing your communication skills in Chapter 4. While there may be some responsibilities you can't off load, there are likely to be many that you can. Remember, it can be a kindness to shift responsibility back to where it belongs - if you always look after other people they don't develop the ability to look after themselves or discover strengths or new sides to themselves.

'My husband's relationship has blossomed with the children since he started taking charge of their Sunday morning activities.'

A characteristic of being a carer to everyone is an inability to ask for help and sympathy yourself. Developing the habit of doing so can bring heart-warming results.

THE HOME ROUTINE

You might not be able to make your employer more responsive, your children less demanding or your partner more sympathetic, but what you do at home is under your control. You set the standards, allocate the time, organise the routine. If you choose to make this a time-consuming priority, at least it's your own choice. You can also choose to streamline it to near nothing. Some people find scrubbing the kitchen floor a therapeutic activity, for others it's just another chore. It's your own feelings that count.

The day to day routine

It can help to introduce a routine if the family faces a frantic early morning rush. For some people this includes packing bags the night before and leaving them by the door, setting breakfast before bed and making sure there are clean clothes ready.

Encourage the family to work as a team. Make it the responsibility of older children to do more for themselves. A routine can help with the evening rush, too. It may be easier if you organise in advance - possibly at the weekend - what everyone is going to eat for supper and who is going to take it out of the freezer. Have set times for homework and a set routine for bath time and bed time. It may sound regimented but it will simply feel structured once you are used to it.

Housework

Again, family team work helps. Divide up the household jobs between you, your partner and older children. The younger the children are when they have their first jobs the better. A calendar on the wall in the kitchen marked with who's doing what and when saves arguments.

If possible, get paid help, even once a week for a few hours - it will be money well spent. A cleaner could do the heavy jobs, or those you really hate such as ironing.

Anticipating and preparing for regular stressful events

If you know that a particular event or time of year is difficult for you, it is worth planning in advance how you can ease the strain. Don't baulk at doing something unconventional at traditional times, such as going out for the Christmas meal or not having all the in-laws over.

Approach other crunchpoints in the same way. If arranging elaborate birthday parties is too much, think laterally. How can you make it nice for the children and easier for you? Young children are often quite happy with smaller events and fewer guests. Older children may want to invite a large group: arranging the party in a sports club where all the organising is done for you is one possibility. On the other hand, a picnic and a game of rounders in the park may be a welcome (and inexpensive) novelty after all those 'organised' parties.

Similarly make sure holidays fulfil their function of relaxing and refreshing you. This will vary according to the ages of your children. As a general rule, however, choosing a holiday that will keep your children busy and amused leaves you freer to unwind. From your point of view aim to make it easy and pleasant for yourself. If domestic pottering is a pleasure for you, self-catering might be bliss. If it is a chore you will feel resentful, which is counter-productive however cheap it is.

The demands of school

Some parents find it helpful to involve their children in fixing a time each day for homework or revision. Be supportive and encouraging in the beginning and at difficult times, and try not to let homework build up into a dreaded daily event. It should, in time, become a natural part of the routine.

At exam time, make sure there is plenty of time to relax as well as revise: winding down is just as important as revising efficiently.

Out-of-school activities

The key here is to restrict them to a manageable level, while encouraging your children in their interests. You may have to concentrate on the ones that are most enjoyed and let others go if the after-school programme has become too hectic for you, your child or a carer. Sharing chauffering with other parents whose children are also involved makes it much easier.

Your involvement in school activities

'There were some things I knew I just had to make time for. I never missed a carol concert or school play, for example. It would have broken my daughter's heart.'

You might have to be strict with yourself and your children on this. There is the phantom 'Everybody', whose father goes on school trips and whose mother bakes cakes for the fete and makes intricate costumes for the school play. You won't want to miss occasions that are important for your children, such as parents' day, and perhaps some sports' days and entertainments, but some things you will have to say no to.

CRISIS MANAGEMENT

Every so often something crops up that makes nonsense of your carefully planned daily routine. This happens to everyone, but if you have children who need looking after as well as work commitments that need attending to then you may well panic. Forethought and planning will help with this. The nature of a crisis is to be unpredictable, but there is one that you know is bound to happen from time to time: illness.

When your children or their regular carers are ill you may want or need to take time off work to care for them yourself. Your employer might not like it, but won't be surprised. In the long-run it is probably in the interests of your employer to be as supportive as possible under these circumstances. Aim to be as professional as possible in estimating how long you will need to be away and in doing what you can to make sure that essential aspects of your job are taken care of.

> 'The twelve months following my wife's death were the most difficult of my life. The company's flexible working policy helped my family pull through - I had time for my children and found that my productivity at work was much higher as a result.'

Sometimes, however, your children might be poorly but not ill, or it is your carer who is sick. In these instances you might feel it is not essential for you to take time off work. This is when you need to be able to call on others to help.

Getting support

A support network of people you can turn to takes the panic out of a crisis. It is usually quite informal (although some people formalise an aspect of it - making an agreement with someone else's nanny to help out for payment at certain times). A good range of support can include the following:

Parents with same-age children
You are likely to meet other new parents when you have your first baby. Working parents often find that these relationships become some of the most enduring.

Neighbours
Close neighbours can be particularly valuable because they are on hand. Those you become friendly with will have plenty of opportunities to get to know you and your children well.

Parents with nannies
If you employ a nanny, she is likely to know other local nannies, who may be able to help out with emergency childcare cover.

Childminders
If you use a childminder check out whether she has ties with a local network of other childminders who help each other out in case of illness.

Working parents group, NCT group or similar
Joining such a group is a useful way of meeting people who live locally and share the same lifestyle. This can be a good way of getting to know people who might be interested in sharing childcare or the school run, or setting up an emergency childcare

register. It also helps just being able to share experiences together.

Though you may not meet them at the school gates you will probably get to know them at weekend parties and school events.

Supporting each other

A network works when it is mutually beneficial. With other parents, for instance, you can offer to take a child to school or invite a child to stay overnight or include other children in weekend actvities. For neighbours without children you can offer to babysit a cat or water the plants while they are away. Beware calling on the good nature of someone who can't say no if you always ask for help and never give anything in return. Swap essential details, such as school, work and doctor's phone numbers, with the people who help you and whom you help.

By combining these recommendations and those in chapters 2 and 4, you can substantially reduce the stress in your life. It also helps to get together with other people for emotional and practical support. The next chapter contains personal experiences from other working parents.

CHECKLIST

1. Devise routines that suit your life style but make it easier.

2. Streamline where you can; cut out non-essential tasks and extras.

3. Get out of the habit of saying yes to everything you are asked to do.

4. Find people who can support you, and who you can help in turn.

5. Face up to the regular events you find stressful and look for practical ways of making them less so.

6. When you are going through a difficult period treat yourself gently.

When home impacts on work:

1. Estimate as accurately as you can how much time it will take.

2. Where possible make contingency plans to cover yourself at work.

3. Tell your employer how long you need off and what your contingency plans are, or take part of your holiday.

7. PERSONAL EXPERIENCES

Pam

Job: self employed, full-time bookkeeper
Childcare: childminder

My biggest source of stress is money, and in particular keeping the cash flowing in the right direction. I'm self employed and work full-time from home. But stopping work to have my son coincided with the recession and really knocked the stuffing out of my business. It has taken me nearly two years to build it back up again. At the same time, we moved to a bigger house to accommodate our larger family, and so we now have larger mortgage payments.

As well as our son, we have a five-year-old daughter and so I have had to pay for a full-time childminder on a regular basis. That has put me under a lot of pressure to bring in a steady and reliable income. It helps that my husband works in local government in a secure job with regular hours.

I feel a constant lack of time to do the things that need to be done. There are particular problems when both my husband and I work on Saturday. We ask friends to look after the children but I feel guilty at not being there for them. Guilt feelings seem to crop up quite frequently and even sometimes encroach into my me-time. I find myself lying in the sauna thinking I ought to be with my children instead of stretched out here.

Four years ago, we went through a very stressful time after my daughter broke her leg. She was two and was in hospital for weeks. We took it in turns to be with her.

My main strategy for coping is coming to terms. I don't worry about the future or what might happen, because I find that worst things usually come from what's totally unpredictable. Worrying is just not worth the effort and acknowledging that has made easier for me to cope with anxieties.

I find friends, allies and networks very helpful. My idea of me-time is getting on to other people's committees. Working is part of my way of creating it too: I have designed my life around my need to work. Much as I love my kids, I find being with them is very stress inducing.

I negotiate time for myself with my husband. If there's a need for one of us to be at home with the children, in case of illness, we talk about who's going to do it. Because he is reasonably senior in his job, he can reschedule his time if he needs to, but he would never say at work that it was because of the children. One of the advantages of being self employed is that I can sometimes arrange my work around the children's demands; I can make myself available for school sports days and occasions that are important to them.

Angela

Job: emergency duty social worker
Childcare: shared with husband and a childminder

As an emergency duty social worker, I work from 6pm to 9am two or three nights a week and do a 24 hour weekend shift from 9am to 9am, about two in five. Arising from that comes some daytime work - meetings to attend and work to do from home. On the night shifts, I could be up all night or able to get as much as four hours sleep.

The most stressful time is when work meets family commitments and this usually happens every evening just before I start work. I try to make sure we're all fed before I go out, and while I'm getting the dining room ready and preparing the dinner, I worry whether my husband will be home on time.

He works from 9am to 5.30pm and we share most of the childcare between us. We have a boy of four who is at nursery school for half a day each day, and a girl of two. My husband dashes in at twenty to six and I start work at six. I hate being late in case people think I can't manage. I refuse to be seen not to be coping with my job. I make sure I do everything fully and I know this puts me under more pressure. I probably make more meetings than my male colleagues and I would never use my children as an excuse for not being there - only if they were ill.

I have a childminder for my daughter for my daytime working hours. I try and arrange to go into the office when she is with the childminder and my son is at nursery. Because I don't work regular daytime hours, I'm constantly having to sort out my childcare. Every week's different.

The weekends can be quite tough. My husband works all week and when I'm on call on Saturday or Sunday, he has all the childcare. Often my son gets fed up that I am working and not able to join in. I find that difficult.

On those weekends, we only have one day together as a family. But when I'm on call, I can be at home, so I am able to spend at least some of the time with the children. I make a phone call, run up to see what they are doing, and then go back to the phone again. My husband is in charge. Until we got used to it, it was very stressful; he would still ask me what to give the children for tea, and so on. I would shout at him: I can't decide, you're in charge now, I'm working. Gradually it has got better.

Because I work such odd hours, time management has become crucial. I live by my diary and the calendar on the wall. Both my husband and I meticulously write down everything we are doing.

And I do make time for myself. It's crucial. I acknowledge that I'm not superhuman and that means I need time for me. I might leave the office, and go for a swim before picking the children up. I'm lucky in being able to make time for myself in the day.

I also feel lucky having a childminder flexible enough to be able to take my child when I ask her. In return, I'm able to be flexible for her, altering the times when I work at home if need be. As a fall back, I have two friends who can help out, and because I am often at home with my own children I can reciprocate by looking after theirs.

For my partner and me this way of living and working has taken some getting used to. It was tough in the beginning but we've worked it out now. I've also trained myself to catch up on missed sleep quite effectively.

Our life is very planned and even our leisure time is mapped out. We miss out a bit on not being able to do things on the spur of the moment. But at the weekends when I don't work, we always plan to do something together: it might be going swimming or to a museum. We want to make the most of our time and it's essential to make time for the family.

Mary

Job: part-time teacher
Childcare: none

Two years ago when I was teaching in a state school I had a much shorter temper than I have now that I have moved into the private sector. If you can guarantee you are going to be pushed, shoved and sworn at for a good part of the day, it gets you geared up before you even arrive.

I teach three mornings a week and have two daughters of 6 and 8. The greatest source of stress has been going through a divorce which is still continuing. It shades my life and has an impact on the way I parent my children. It's hard not having anyone to bounce ideas off and if you have a problem with one of your children, there is no one with a sympathetic ear to listen. There is nobody else to rely on for school runs or to go out for a pint of milk if I have forgotten it. I have to be all things to all people.

There is a constant battle over finances. My former husband holds the purse strings. I want to do my best for the children but money is always a problem.

I feel in a constant state of emotional turmoil over their visits to him. I dread the sense of being a wicked mother keeping them from their darling father but it feels as though they're being taken away from me when they go to him, and I spend all afternoon waiting until they come back.

It's difficult meeting people and especially people in the same situation. I can't join a babysitting circle because I can't reciprocate. As I don't live near relatives, it is almost impossible for me to get any time to myself. Friends tend to be more reluctant to help single parents because of the reciprocation problem and the worry that you might become a permanent burden. You do learn who your real friends are.

The way I cope is by limiting things. The buck stops with me and I try to be realistic about how much I can take on and what I can cope with. I have to be in control, and I recognise, and make sure that others do too, that I can only be in one place at one time. At the weekends I now insist on having a lie-in and I have trained my children not to bother me before 9am.

Last year, I was under a great deal of stress and I decided to start going for a massage once a week. I went every week for 3 months. I couldn't really afford it but it helped considerably. It was physically relaxing and there was a sense of luxury in being attended to.

In some ways my part-time job is the perfect job for me, especially now I've changed schools. It means I don't need any childcare and I have time to do all the domestic things I need. I feel burdened with responsibility at home, but have none at school. Only the report times are stressful. And I get an income and have colleagues.

Paul

Job: charity director
Childcare: daily nanny, playgroup for three-year-old

We have three boys aged three, six and eight. My wife and I both now work full-time, but with long holidays, part paid, part unpaid, thanks to flexible employers. The content of our work (in children's organisations) makes us sensitive about conflicts between working full-time on children's issues and giving our children the time they have a right to. Luckily, and rightly, it makes our employers sensitive too.

After each birth, Rebecca had five months paid leave, of which she took all after each birth. Each time, I took six weeks off, so that as a "new" family we had a solid period together. My employer allowed three weeks paternity leave, and did not oppose additional unpaid leave. Rebecca staged her return to work, increasing from one day a week up to four days a week over a six month period. I was allowed to work full-time over four long days, leaving me with one full day as well as weekends with our son. Close friends provided our first daycare, acting as " unofficial childminder" for the other three days. The same arrangement continued around and after the birth of our second son. When our friends left the country, we found an "official" childminder, but our children, who had regarded our friends' house as an attractive second home, were clearly less happy (tearful separations for the first time). So we advertised for a non-live-in nanny.

Soon after our eldest started school (at four in our area), our third son was born. We again took a period off together immediately after the birth, but by this time I had returned to five day working succumbing, probably stupidly, to workaholism.

Now our youngest is three, he attends playgroup four mornings a week, and the other two are in the local infants/junior school. We have our second, wonderful nanny, whom they clearly love. She organises a busy social life for them with friends after playgroup/ school. Rebecca and I both work full-time, except that I pick them up from school on Fridays. We take turns taking them to school in the morning and one or other of us gets back by 6pm to start the bedtime rituals of games, bath, books. They last to 8pm and we then have a little "adult" time before dropping very early into bed ...

For three years now we have resolved to spend most of the summer and all of the Easter holiday with the children, as well as half-term weeks: this means adding unpaid leave to our five/six weeks paid holiday. Again, our employers have been flexible, and it seems a very good compromise, although it does mean very pressurised work periods in between.

Chris

Job: full-time engineer
Childcare: workplace nursery

Sue works for the same company as I do which makes life easier as we both live with the same company culture and understand when pressures are on at work. On the other hand, now we have a family, we also share the pressures of caring for our children and try to share the taking and fetching to nursery as much as possible.

Although the company is more tolerant towards mothers needing to leave promptly at the end of the day, I find that there is still a lot of pressure from my work colleagues to stay late. Somehow its still not OK for men to be seen to share the responsibility for children. Because our two children attend a nursery, it is essential that they are collected on time - they don't like to be last and nor are we popular with the staff if we're late.

We were lucky enough to get our first baby into the newly opened company nursery but it was touch and go if the second would get a place and at one moment, when we were told there were no available baby places, we were faced with the problem of having two different forms of childcare or moving our older toddler from the nursery. Now we are worrying about how to juggle one toddler at a nursery where we work, with our older daughter starting at the local school near our home. The childcare problem never seems to go away: the goal posts just keep shifting.

I have had two major stresses so far. First, my wife had to go into hospital for bed-rest shortly before our second child was born. Coping with work, a fretting toddler and getting to visit Sue in hospital each day was tough but it would have been impossible without the security of the day nursery for us all. Second, I have been working under the threat of redundancy for the past year as our department is being 'downsized' as part of general cuts. Having this hanging over us for so long has been a constant worry, especially now we have children - but at least I have them to cheer me up when work is getting me down.

Stella

Job: full-time secretary
Childcare: out-of-school club

My partner walked out on me shortly before I had Sam and I've brought him up alone since then (he's six now). I have been with the same employer during this time and always found them very supportive - even when Sam had asthma as a baby and I frequently had to take him to hospital. I had a supportive line manager to thank at the time but the company now has a proper policy about time off to care for sick children as well as an emergency care scheme.

I can now look back on the years before Sam started school and, while they were really hard, both financially and exhausting, I'm glad I stuck at my work. I'm currently undergoing training to step into my supervisor's position when she goes on maternity leave and I would never have got this far had I given up.

In some ways, I would like to be in control of our lives and manage my own money rather than having someone else to worry about and tidy up after. We never see Sam's father and I don't miss him after the way he walked out, but I do worry about Sam as he gets older.

Childcare has been a constant headache, finding it and being able to pay for someone reliable. We moved a couple of times when

Sam was small which didn't help but things are more settled and, with the help of the company childcare information officer, I've found a school near to our new home which has an out-of-school club linked to it.

Now Sam is over all the childhood illnesses and at regular school, I am finding life less of a mad scramble. The club is open until 6pm in term-time and from 9am to 6pm in school holidays so I no longer have panics about what to do in the summer vacation as I did before he moved to this school.

The worst part of being a lone parent for me is having time to myself without feeling guilty. I feel I must put everything into work to keep my job and spend all my home time with Sam. Going out - even to attend a school PTA meeting - is very difficult because I don't know many people where I live and babysitters are so expensive. Socialising, apart from having friends round, is a rare treat. The thing that kept me sane when Sam was young was belonging to a local working mothers group which had weekend playgroups I could bring Sam to. I'm still in touch with one of the mums I met then and we meet up occasionally at weekends with the kids and compare notes on how we're coping with the latest dramas!

Rupika

Job: full-time shop manageress
Childcare: au pair

When Danny was little, I gave up work as it wasn't worth the money by the time I paid for childcare. Recently, when my former boss offered me the job of managing his new shop, I took the opportunity as my husband's computer job is not so secure any longer.

Danny has just started school and I'm glad I had time to settle him in before going back to full-time work. My hours are long: I work in the West End and don't get home much before 7pm. We have an au pair to take and fetch him from school and give him his tea, and then my husband usually gets home around 6pm. It's strange having an au pair sharing our home and having to think about another young person: you forget that even though they are coming to care for your child, they sometimes need support themselves. On the other hand its a great relief to know that there is someone always there to fetch Danny from school and play with him in his own home.

Brian and I try to share Danny's upbringing as much as possible and his family live nearby which is a great help - most of the time! Sometimes we disagree about how to discipline him when he's naughty and I have my own strong views about things like table manners which are different to those of Brian's family. These differences of opinion seem to be a greater stress than anything else! If anything, being back at working and having to pull together more as a team has improved the time when we can all relax together - maybe we all appreciate it more now.

| Barbara | **Job: full-time student**
Childcare: childminder and partner |

One of the difficulties of retraining after having stopped work for 12 years is that you have a loss of confidence in your abilities. And it's hard to leave your children for the first time - mine are now 11, 9 and 6 and I feel concerned that I am not able to be there for them as much as I was.

I'm training to be a social worker which involves going to lectures, doing workplace placements, a lot of course reading and essay writing. I find the work, especially the placements, emotionally demanding and very stressful. Sometimes after a harrowing day, I can't sleep at night. I always need a spell of time to myself when I get in. Fortunately my husband and children are very supportive. They can see that I am committed to completing my training, and they help out as much as they can.

Our family life has changed completely. We've made a lot of practical adjustments. I used to clean the house and cook nice meals. Now the house doesn't get a thorough clean until the holidays and we eat a lot of fast food. I have taken on a cleaner once a week, for the first time ever. I still try and do as many jobs as I can first thing in the morning. Because we all tend to go off in different directions in the morning, we have to plan this time very carefully: make sure the car is running properly and that our various machines are all working.

My dog doesn't get walked as much as he used to, and now that I can't reciprocate by helping friends with their children, I pay a childminder to look after my youngest son after-school until I collect him at 6pm. I pay her the standard childminding fee. My older children are away at school during the week.

It's important for me to have clearly defined family times and work times, and if I can't keep them separate, I feel the stress starting to build up. Because my weekdays are so long and full, I try to keep the weekends free for the family.

There are huge pluses for me in having started this retraining. I get a great deal of satisfaction from doing the course work and look forward to the prospect of qualifying and getting a job. I feel that the years of hard grind with the children are well past and now that my older children are starting to develop their own lives, they only need me as a babysitter.

I feel that what I'm doing is quite selfish even though my children are very clearly still my first priority. I find it more important than ever to make time for myself. Now it is usually at the weekend, and I might go to a concert with a friend. I counter the worry about my abilities with a great sense of pride in what I am managing to achieve, combining working and having children.

Lesley

Job: part-time projects coordinator
Childcare: mother and shared nanny

My mother looks after my 10 month old son one day a week; for the other two and a half days I work, I share a nanny. She likes to keep that contact and puts herself out, changing her own work commitments, to make sure that she can do it. She'll also step in at odd moments if I need help. She lives locally and we have a good relationship which is crucial for this kind of arrangement to work well.

When my son was born we were living with her and she interfered quite a lot with the way I did things. I found it hard to hold my tongue sometimes. We still occasionally fall out over how warmly he should be dressed, but otherwise everything has calmed down and we hardly have any disagreements. My partner and I now live in our own flat and she comes here and picks him up.

I absolutely trust her to give him the sort of attention I want him to have, and to play with him in the way I would. And of course I feel confident of her love for him. It is a very positive thing in my life having her help out and I know he's totally safe when he's with her.

I don't pay her anything - neither of us would dream of it I'm sure, and I have no worries about her finding it all too much. She is in her early fifties and still sprightly. If I have any concerns about him - if he's teething for example, I can phone her in the middle of the day and find out how he is. Talking to her really reassures me.

Lorraine

Job: shift worker, telephone answering service
Childcare: playgroup and shared with husband

I have twins who are 3 and I work because we need the money. My husband works for his father and their business has been badly affected by the recession. We moved a year ago into a bigger house and didn't realise then how badly the mortgage payments would affect us.

I have quite an interesting job, working at a computerised switching centre that provides an answering service for doctors. It's quite quiet and one of the few jobs I could find that pays enough to be worthwhile. Before I had the twins I was a secretary in direct marketing but I didn't want to return there after having them: at that time we had no financial worries. I worked from home for a charity for nothing.

I've recently changed from doing the night shift to doing an evening shift from 5.30pm to 10pm, three evenings a week. I really suffered from lack of sleep before and found myself taking it out on the kids. I was always snapping at my husband as well and I used to hate going to work. He was so tired, he'd go to bed at 9.30pm, just as I was going out. The children have me all day, then I wolf down my tea in 10 minutes and go to work as soon as Steven gets home. He works on Saturdays and so I can never work during the day. Recently the twins have started going to playgroup which means I can get things done in the house in the morning. Having twins makes everything like going swimming more difficult, but we get out as much as we can. I am on the committee of the local twins club.

Our social life has to be fitted in around the evenings I am not working. We never go out on Saturdays or Sundays because I often work one of them and sometimes both. We get paid more for working at the weekend. Getting a babysitter is expensive so on the whole I relax by doing simple things like having a nice bath.

8. USEFUL ADDRESSES

Childcare

Daycare Trust
Wesley House, 4 Wild Court, London WC2B 5AU (071 405 5617)
Research and information on childcare and community based
resource and referral services in partnership with employers.

Kids' Clubs Network
279 - 281 Whitechapel Road, London E1 1BY (071 247 3009).
Promotes out-of-school and holiday care for children up to 12;
useful literature on setting up schemes.

National Childminding Association
8 Masons Hill, Bromley, Kent BR2 9EX (081 464 6164).
Promotes standards and interests of childminders. Useful literature for both minders and parents. Has draft contract.

Pre-School Playgroups Association
61-63 Kings Cross Road, London WC1X 9LL (071 833 0991).
Information on local playgroups, some with extended hours to
suit working parents.

Working for Childcare
77 Holloway Road, London N7 8JZ (071 700 0281)
Campaigns for all forms of good quality childcare and advises on
workplace schemes.

Working Mothers Association
77 Holloway Road, London N7 8JZ (071 700 5771).
Practical information on all forms of childcare for individuals and
employers. Also has a network of local support groups (see
publications in next section).

Health and therapies

The British Association for Counselling
1 Regent Place, Rugby, Warwickshire CV21 2PJ (0788 578328).
Has names of qualified counsellors.

The British Association of Psychotherapists
37 Mapesbury Road, London NW2 4HJ (081 452 9823).
Names of qualified psychotherapists are also available from GPs
or other therapy units.

The British Complementary Medicine Association
St Charles Hospital, Exmoor Street, London W10 6DZ
(081 964 1205).

Institute for Complementary Medicine
PO Box 194, London SE16 1QZ (write with sae).

Relaxation for Living
168-170 Oatlands Drive, Weybridge, Surrey KT13 9ET
(0932 858355).
Teaches stress management through physical relaxation and
improved health.

The UK Council for Psychotherapy
Regent's College, Inner Circle, Regent's Park, London NW1 4NS
(071 487 7554).
A new national register of qualified and accredited psychotherapists.

Home stresses

Exploring Parenthood
Latimer Education Centre, 194 Freston Road, London W10 6TT
(081 960 1678).
Workshops and discussion groups to explore the problems and
pleasures of being a parent.

Gingerbread
35 Wellington Street, London WC2E 7BN (071 240 0953).
Support for single parents and their children.

The National Childbirth Trust
Alexandra House, Oldham Terrace, London W3 6NH
(081 992 8637).
Provides local support groups and many useful leaflets.

National Council for the Divorced and Separated
13 High Street, Little Shelford, Cambridge CB2 5ES
(0533 700595).

The National Council for One Parent Families
255 Kentish Town Road, London NW5 2LX (071 267 1361).
Research, advice and parliamentary lobbying to improve every
aspect of life for one parent families. Supports provision of day
care facilities for working parents.

National Family Conciliation Council
The Shaftesbury Centre, Percy Street, Swindon SN2 2AZ
(0793 514 055).
For couples going through separation or divorce. Helps arbitrate
with arrangements that need to be worked out, especially over
children.

Parent Network
44-46 Caversham Road, London NW5 2DS (071 485 8535).
For information on local support and education groups, known as
Parent-Link.

Parentline
(0268 757077).
A network of groups for parents under stress. Also runs helplines
and some drop-in centres.

Parents Anonymous
(071 263 8918 and 081 668 4805)
A telephone helpline for all parents under stress.
Relate
National Marriage Guidance Council, Herbert Gray College,
Little Church Street, Rugby CV21 3AP (0788 573241).

Scottish Marriage Guidance Council
105 Hanover Street, Edinburgh EH2 1DG (031 225 5006).

Work stresses

Equal Opportunities Commission
Overseas House, Quay Street, Manchester M3 3HN
(061 833 9244).
Useful for statistical information on childcare as well as more obvious equal opportunities work.

Home Run
Active Information, PO Box 2841, London W6 (tel: 081 741 2440; fax : 081 846 9244).
A new subscription magazine for people working from home.

International Stress Management Association
South Bank University, LPSS, 103 Borough Road, London SE1 OAA.
Written enquiries only. Provides information about and training in all aspects of stress management.

Maternity Alliance
15 Britannia Street, London WC1X 9JP (071 837 1265).
Provides information on maternity rights and services.

New Ways to Work
309 Upper Street, London N1 2TY (071 226 4026).
Information on flexible working and job-sharing.

Own Base
68 First Avenue, Bush Hill Park, Enfield, EN1 1BN (081 363 0808).
A support network and newsletter for people who work from home.

Women Returners Network
8 John Adam Street, London WC2N 6EZ (071 839 8188).
Provides information on courses to update you in your field, self assessment and career planning.

Parents at Work/Working Mothers Association
77 Holloway Road, London N7 8JZ (071 700 5771).
Information on 'family friendly' policies to help parents in the workplace. Support via a network of local groups.

USEFUL PUBLICATIONS

About Time - The Revolution in Work and Family Life
Patricia Hewitt. IPPR/Rivers Oram Press, £9.95.

Best Companies for Women Scarlett MccGwire. Pandora.
£7.99.

Coping with stress at work Jacqueline M Atkinson. Thorsons.
£5.99.

The Family Friendly Employer, Examples from Europe
Christine Hogg and Lisa Harker. Daycare Trust in association
with Families and Work Institute, New York. 071 405 5617.

Living with Stress Cary L Cooper, Rachel D Cooper, Lynn E
Eaker. Penguin Health. £5.99.

Lyn Marshall's Instant Stress Cure Vermilion/Ebury Press.
£7.99.

Massage Therapy Adam J Jackson. Optima. £5.99.

The Mental Health Media Council 380 Harrow Road, London
W9 2HU (071 286 2346) Has two useful listings: a video
directory of over 400 titles on Women and Well-Being for £6
and a leaflet, Managing Stress, which lists over 200 titles on
stress and stress management for £4.

The MIND Information Unit, 22 Harley Street, London W1N
2ED   (071 637 0791) Has a booklist and list of teachers for
assertiveness training.

The Positive Woman Gael Lindenfield. Thorsons. £5.99.

Relax: Dealing with stress Murray Watts and Cary L Cooper.
BBC Health UK. £5.99.

Stress and Relaxation Jane Madders. Optima. £7.99.

Understanding Stress Which? Consumer Guide. Consumers'
Association and Hodder & Stoughton. £9.99.

PARENTS AT WORK/
WORKING MOTHERS ASSOCIATION

Publications

Carer's Contract
Ready-made, incorporating all areas you should cover when
employing nanny/mother's help. Blanks to fill in your own details.
Free to WMA members.

Employers Guide to Childcare
Written for managers and task-groups, this 132 page book
examines the many ways employers can help working parents.
Examples of workplace initiatives from over 80 employers in the
UK include childcare benefits, workplace nurseries, career break
schemes and job-sharing. Costs and benefits are assessed.

Information Leaflets
WMA: Who are we?
Why Your Company Should Belong (Corporate Membership)
Setting up a Local Group
About WMA Workshops

Maternity Pack
A useful, comprehensive guide to help women get the best from
their maternity leave. Includes *The Working Parents Handbook*
and *WMA Newsletter* plus list of local WMA support groups,
maternity rights calendar and other material. For individuals or
for companies who want to give packs as a cost-effective way to
encourage women to return to work.

Newsletter
For working parents, this is a magazine style publication, full of
news, information and personal experiences. Free with annual
membership or may be purchased individually.

Returners Handbook
Essential information to help women get started with planning a return to work, including when, plus careers advice and training courses. Also, looking for work, filling in application forms, interviews and childcare information. New in 1994.

The Working Parents Handbook
A practical guide to the alternatives in childcare from childminder to nanny to nursery to out-of-school schemes. Factors to consider in choosing childcare. How to find and interview carers, pay tax and National Insurance. As well as useful information on parental rights under The Children Act 89, the book also contains helpful hints on preparing yourself for being a 'working parent!' and persuading your employer to be 'family friendly'. Revised annually.

Courses

One-day Workshops
Including information pack plus lunch and refreshments. Open to individuals or to companies who wish to send employees. WMA can also run courses in-house for employers.

Taking Maternity Leave
Work and pregnancy (organising your time effectively, managing stress, understanding maternity benefits), relationships and self (relaxation, changes), planning after the birth (new emotions, deciding on childcare).

Back to Work
Being a working mother (managing the balance, dealing with fatigue, a five year plan), mixed feelings (separating from your child, finding your confidence, realising your ambitions), childcare (interviewing carers, settling your child).

Implementing Family Friendly Policies
An introduction to family friendly policies for equal opportunities and line managers.